PRAISE FOR *THE APPLE AND THE SHADY TREE*

"An honest, funny, and thorough reflection on a complicated family. The memoir is full of details, anecdotes, and short profiles of colorful characters . . . Though the author's memoir delivers on its promise to present a realistic look at her father's ties to the Genovese crime family, the true success of the work is how well it encapsulates a time and place: New York of the '60s, '70s, and '80s.

—*Kirkus Reviews*

"Ms. Goldberg (tells) her story with the slant that a childhood surrounded by crime and mischief-making was as normal as every other nearby household—despite its dysfunctionality . . . it was hard to stop reading . . . I highly recommend *The Apple and the Shady Tree: The Mafia, My Family, and Me* to any person wanting an eye-opening and entertaining picture of the Mob."

—*The Art is Alive Magazine*

"An introspective look at the author's dysfunctional family, recounting mob-related murders and stories of mob members . . . in 1960s and '70s Brooklyn. Beyond these *Goodfellas*-esque anecdotes, Goldberg's memoir is also a candid look at her family's history of mental health issues and her complicated relationship with her father."

—*PEOPLE*.COM

"Using riveting chronological vignettes from her own life—some horrifying, some hilarious, thanks to her sharp wit—Goldberg takes readers into the corrupt, chaotic, and sometimes glamorous world of organized crime and reveals how the mafia, who were her father's closest friends and business associates, wreaked havoc on her family as a child and her mental health as an adult."

—*Broadway World*

"*The Apple and the Shady Tree* [is] a terrific book."

—*Jewish Post and News*

THE APPLE AND
THE SHADY TREE

THE APPLE AND THE SHADY TREE

THE MAFIA, MY FAMILY, AND ME

LISA NOVICK GOLDBERG

O'Possum Press

Published by O'Possum Press

Edited and designed by Girl Friday Productions
www.girlfridayproductions.com

Design: Paul Barrett
Image credits: cover © Shutterstock/Bonitas

ISBN: 978-0-578-58513-0

Copyright registration number: TXu 2-123-155

To my father, whose life lessons, both good and bad, taught with intention or otherwise, made me strong.

In each journey of your life you must be where you are. You may only be passing through on your way to somewhere else seemingly more important—nevertheless, there is purpose in where you are right now.

Bringing Heaven Down to Earth: Meditations and Everyday Wisdom from the Teachings of the Rebbe, Menachem Schneerson, Compiled by Tzvi Freeman

INTRODUCTION

They say that "the apple doesn't fall far from the tree." I like to think that this McIntosh took a long roll into another orchard, but I'm not sure. I'll let you judge.

This is a book about my family, the Novicks, who were at best described as "unusual." It is about my complicated relationship with my father, whose closest friends just happened to be the bosses of the Genovese crime family. It is about my search to find myself after having spent a lifetime straddling two very distinct worlds: one as an upper-middle-class suburban girl who attended elite schools, ran in privileged circles, and identified strongly with her Judaism, and the other as a sort of Mafia princess whose upbringing gave access to another kind of elitism and privilege and landed me in front of a grand jury.

The story is told from my perspective. You are introduced to my father, Herbert Novick, born into a poor Jewish family in 1928 in the rough-and-tough Brownsville neighborhood of Brooklyn, made infamous as the home of Murder Inc. A job as a teenager on the Brooklyn dockyards changed his fate when he met the men who became his lifelong friends—the men who then went on to become the capos of the powerful Genovese family. It was then that Herbie Novick morphed into "John" or "Johnny" or "Big Johnny Novick."

You will meet his bride, my stunning but deeply troubled mother, who was a formidable match in their explosive fifty-three-year marriage. Their genetic shortcomings and poor choices created a chaotic home for my sister and me, characterized by anger and fear, disappointment and confusion. I have been far luckier than my sister, who could never overcome the abuse of being used as a pawn in our parents' battles.

Through chronological vignettes, both very funny and profoundly sad, I take you on my journey from early childhood in Brooklyn, to the wealthy Jewish ghetto known as the Five Towns of Long Island where I grew up, to my adulthood, with its twists and turns, challenges and triumphs.

Beginning with a murder, I introduce you to the real-life Goodfellas who came in and out of my life courtesy of my father's role as a moneymaker for the Genovese family. We will visit the Mafia-infused worlds of the casinos of glitzy 1960s, 1970s, and 1980s Las Vegas and Atlantic City; the boxing industry; Manhattan's iconic Garment Center; the pre-MTV record industry; the restaurants where mob business deals were made and celebrated; and a corrupt boutique bank that was tied to a mob murder.

So join me, it's quite a ride!

CHAPTER 1

THE MURDER:
THE BEGINNING
OF THE END

On Sunday, August 9, 1987, I was twenty-nine years old. My now ex-husband, Mark, and I had returned to our New York City apartment from a relaxing summer weekend on Long Island. I was getting my things together in preparation for the next day's work at the bank while the ten p.m. metro news played on the TV.

"Oh my God!" I screamed. "Mark, hurry! You gotta see this."

The newscaster was reporting the lead story:

"An execution-style murder was carried out yesterday evening at Bravo Sergio, a restaurant on Second Avenue and Seventy-Fifth Street in Manhattan. The dead man has been identified as Irwin Schiff, a six-foot-four, 350-pound millionaire businessman who had been living in the penthouse of the St. James, a luxury building on the East Side. Mr. Schiff reportedly had ties to the Mafia.

"According to eyewitnesses, the assailant entered the restaurant through the back door, which we are told is normally locked; approached Mr. Schiff, who was dining with a younger blonde woman; and shot him in the head. The assailant then fled through the same back door. Terrified diners, including Schiff's dinner companion, fled the restaurant through the front door.

"Police are asking for your help in identifying the woman who had been with Schiff this evening. She was last seen getting into a taxi at the front of the restaurant."[1]

Irwin Schiff was one of my father's best friends du jour. For the past couple of years, my father had gushed to his friends, my mother, and me about the very smart, very friendly man who appeared to have unlimited money and connections in varied business and social circles. I had met Irwin for the first time just a few weeks before the shooting, when I'd gone to dinner with him and my parents at Bravo Sergio.

In January 1987, just seven months prior to the homicide, my father had told me that his friends Irwin Schiff and Domenic Rabuffo had opened a boutique bank called First Inter-County Bank (FICB). The bank was in an office suite at 489 Fifth Avenue across from the New York Public Library. I had been looking to change from my current job and asked him to see if there might be any positions available to me. I had no idea what I could offer a bank, but back in the day, I was so unchartered that anything was fair game. I had no career goals at that time, despite having a master's degree in international affairs from Columbia University, and believed that I would learn something important from any job, regardless of the industry. I had gotten married in December 1986, and I anticipated that my

---

1. The details for this news report were gathered from Michael Daly's "The Fat Man: The Life and High Times of Irwin Schiff," *New York Magazine*, October 19, 1987.

husband, Mark, was going to be a successful personal injury attorney and that it wouldn't be long before we moved to the suburbs to start a family. I also liked the idea that the bank was within walking distance from our apartment and that it was a nine-to-five job.

My father took me to the bank to interview with Phil Wolitzer, the chief financial officer. Phil was a short, soft-spoken, older Jewish man with glasses who seemed intelligent and very professional. I sat in his office, and we talked about my résumé and the fact that he was looking for an assistant. As a CPA and professor of business, he was impressed by the schools I had attended, my self-applauded strong organizational skills, my conservative manner, and my enthusiasm. He told me that a background in banking wasn't necessary for the position; I would learn what I needed along the way.

Phil then introduced me to the bank president, Tiberiu "Tibi" Horovitz, and the vice president, Jack Graff. Neither fit the stereotype of bank executives; they were very relaxed and casual in their dress and demeanor. Tibi joked that he was surprised I was Johnny Novick's daughter. I understood the humor, we all clicked, and I was hired.

So many of my father's friends were eccentric or had lifestyles that tight-roped the line of legality. I lived with concerns that my connection to them would somehow put me in jeopardy; however, these concerns did not override my decisions in the past to ask for help when seeking employment. My new position with FICB gave me a sense of calm and security despite the connection to my father. First, I rationalized that a bank was bound by federal regulations, so there would be no room for any creativity. Second, the bank bunch were all accredited professionals. Third, the top guys were all Jewish. I trusted the common sense and integrity of anyone who left the office early on Fridays to be home in time for Shabbos (Sabbath) dinner. Mr. Graff was an Orthodox Jew; he even wore a yarmulke! I was going to be working with respected people whom I could learn from. Boy, was I naive.

I was determined to make this job a go and threw myself into the role. I even dressed the part of the conservative young female banker, complete with men's tailored oxford shirts from Brooks Brothers, below-the-knee skirts, sensible but stylish low-heeled pumps, and a bob hairstyle. The bob was perhaps the most absurd part of my costume, being that the cut was not suited for my frizzy, unruly hair. I looked like the *Saturday Night Live* character Roseanne Roseannadanna! I topped off the bank trainee look with a leather briefcase that carried nothing but the *New York Times* and mints. I didn't even recognize myself in the mirror!

I spent the first few months on the job trying to learn and impress. I bothered Wolitzer to give me projects, but he was often too busy to assign me anything substantive. One of my projects was to go through clients' files to determine which legally required bank documents were missing, such as signature cards, proof of incorporation, detailed loan documentation, financial statements, and so on. I was surprised to find that only a small number of the files were complete; most were lacking documents, and many were empty files devoid of any corporate paperwork whatsoever. It appeared that the bank had worked backward in its loan process: money was given to the client prior to the proper intake of information that would determine credit worthiness. I don't recall having much luck with the project; the files remained incomplete, and no one seemed too concerned to have the situation corrected.

I had met Domenic "Dom" Rabuffo prior to my arrival at the bank. He looked like he had walked off the set of a Hollywood Mafia movie, his attire and persona carefully orchestrated for public consumption and his own adoration. He was always immaculately dressed. He wore expensive-looking leather shoes, a ring, a necklace, cuff links, and cologne, and he carried a beautiful leather briefcase. His distinguishing feature was his hair; he had a shock of white in his carefully blow-dried black hair that made him look like a cross between Elvis Presley and the amorous cartoon skunk Pepé Le Pew. One day I could not help myself and asked him if the white was courtesy of nature or his barber. "Real," he said. I wasn't convinced.

Domenic was a frequent visitor to FICB as he had been a shareholder in the holding company that controlled FICB until 1986.[2] In early 1987, Domenic's only connection to the bank appeared to be as vice president of the Luis Electrical Contracting Corporation of Long Island City, perhaps FICB's largest account. Luis Electrical had been a major contractor in New York with projects such as the Jacob K. Javits Convention Center.[3] Dom spent many hours in Tibi's office behind closed doors.

It was obvious that Dom and Tibi were good friends in addition to business associates. In the bank's public areas, they could be heard talking about their frequent social outings together with their wives to some of New York City's hottest restaurants and weekend excursions on Dom's forty-two-foot cabin cruiser. I remember feeling oddly envious of them; they seemed to have a lot of fun toys, and they knew how to enjoy them.

By contrast, I have no recollection of Irwin Schiff having visited FICB while I was there, even though he had his own office in the suite. Because space was limited when I arrived at the bank, I was given temporary use of Schiff's office. He had invested $35,000 for a 2.5 percent share of GHW Holding Company (Graff, Horovitz, Wolitzer), which owned FICB. As

---

2. Leonard Buder, "Man Arrested in Loan Fraud Is Said to Be US Informant," *New York Times*, March 12, 1988.
3. Craig Wolff, "Fraud Arrest Is Linked to Murder of a Millionaire," *New York Times*, March 11, 1988.

a partner, Schiff automatically became a member of the bank's board of advisers.

Schiff was known as a flashy millionaire businessman, though no one was sure how he earned his purported $20 million net worth. He claimed that he had owned an entertainment production company, had been a fight promoter with Don King, worked for the CIA, and maintained close ties with the Mafia. He was known to have a controlling interest in Luis Electrical and was a silent partner in Roadworks, a luxury-car-leasing company on Long Island. Schiff was also thought to be a partner in the deluxe Georgian Hotel on Lake George (frequented by mobsters who attended the nearby Saratoga races in August), where he docked his $500,000 cigarette speedboat, and a partner in the China Club, a trendy nightspot on Manhattan's Upper West Side. He lived in a $13,000-per-month penthouse apartment in the St. James on the East Side. He had rented luxury homes in Quogue, Palm Beach, and Fort Lauderdale, where he threw parties frequented by prominent people from a variety of industries. He had a stretch Mercedes limo with a driver and a vintage Stutz Bearcat. He was an extravagant tipper.[4] To sum it up, he left a giant footprint wherever he went.

My father seemed to be extremely impressed with Irwin's wealth and would gush to me and my mom about the man's successes. I found my father's behavior to be immature, yet I also found myself getting pulled into the glamour that surrounded Schiff. My dad would say:

"Lisa, do you know the China Club? All the stars go there. Just tell me when you want to go with your friends. You don't have to wait in line, you'll get right in, and Irwin will make arrangements for you to meet any celebrities who are there." I

---

4. Daly, "The Fat Man."

never took him up on the offer, but I did pass the invitation on to my friends.

"Lisa, Irwin has a beautiful limo. Irwin says that he'll let us use it whenever we want. He's got a heart of gold, Lisa. He's a nice man. Your mother can't stand him. She says something's not right about him. What does she know?" I never did take up this offer.

"Lisa, why don't you and Mark go up to the Georgian Hotel in Lake George? It's beautiful up there! You won't have to pay anything for the room, and there's a restaurant in the hotel that's great! Everything will be comped. You really should go. He'll have the captain of his cigarette boat take you around the lake." I did take him up on this last offer. In August 1986 Mark and I and our friends Laurie and Larry spent a weekend at the simple but lovely hotel and took advantage of all that we were offered.

When Mark and I decided that we wanted to buy our first car, my father insisted that we get it from Roadworks, the company of which Schiff was a partner. Dad claimed, as he frequently did, that we would get the best price if we just used his contacts and stopped trying to prove something by doing things on our own. Mark, who had quickly learned that dealing with my father was a guaranteed headache, protested. Dad won and we bought the car, a very simple, boxy (but safe) Volvo from Roadworks. It arrived weeks after it was promised, causing lots of arguments between Mark and me and my father and me. When would I ever learn?

My father wasn't the only one who was mesmerized by Irwin Schiff. The sentiment was shared by many others who knew him, including the world-renowned fashion photographer Francesco Scavullo, the actress Marisa Berenson, Brooke Shields and her mother, a variety of movers and shakers in the entertainment and business worlds, and a bevy of aspiring

models and starlets from whom Schiff asked nothing in return
for his promises to get their careers started.

***

After Schiff's murder, things really heated up at the bank.
When I arrived for work on Monday morning, August 10, 1987,
things were already in turmoil. Investigators lost no time in
examining the bank's existing relationship with the deceased
Mr. Schiff. Soon after the bank opened in 1985, bank regulators terminated his position as a member of the advisory
board when they discovered that Schiff had a previous criminal record. It was also determined at that time that Schiff had
filed the required bank documents using a false Social Security
number. Investigators also wanted to know the extent of the
relationship between Schiff and his buddy Domenic Rabuffo.[5]

During the week after the murder, members of the bank's
board of advisers, including Averell Harriman Jr., called me
into what had been Schiff's office at the bank and asked me
questions:

"How did you come to work at the bank?"

"Did your father suggest that you get a job at the bank?"

"How did you know Irwin Schiff?"

"How did you know Domenic Rabuffo?"

"What type of work have you been doing for the bank?"

I answered all their questions as best I could, and they
seemed satisfied that I was not planted at the bank to further
anyone's agenda. Investigators set up shop in the bank to con-
duct interviews with the bank's executives and the staff and
to begin a thorough investigation of Schiff's connections to
various individuals and companies that were bank customers. I was soon put to work assisting the bank regulators with
their investigation. As the liaison, I provided the investigators

---

5. Buder, "Man Arrested in Loan Fraud Is Said to Be US Informant."

with copies of the documents that they requested, including many of the incomplete customer loan files. I helped the bank comply with the memorandum of understanding that outlined the regulators' demands for compliance in order to keep FICB open.

The atmosphere in the bank continued to be extremely tense for months after the murder. I was miserable and wanted to quit, but I didn't. I developed a ridiculous but all-too-real-to-me paranoia, believing that if I left the bank, investigators would think that I had something to hide. I made it very well known that I was a member of Team Investigator!

Mr. Wolitzer called me into his office one afternoon and asked if I planned to change my surname to Goldberg rather than keep my maiden name. I asked why, and he responded, "You might want to get rid of the Novick part; you'll be better off."

The well-meaning advice left me numb with worry. Was my father involved in all of this? What was coming?

While police investigators worked on finding Schiff's killer, bank investigators worked on trying to untangle the web of relationships between Schiff, Rabuffo, and FICB.

Well, it turned out that my mother's suspicions about Schiff were correct: he was a fraud, a con man, and a crook. As for being a partner in the China Club and the Georgian Hotel, the true owners of both argued this claim. The $20 million Schiff purported to have in net worth? His accountant claimed that large sums of money had always moved through Schiff's accounts, but no properties or assets could be found in his name. He had also served time in jail for the interstate transport of forged checks, and he was under investigation for tax evasion.[6]

---

6. Joseph F. Sullivan, "Tapes Tell How Schiff Was Murdered," *New York Times*, April 16, 1989.

One week after Irwin Schiff was killed, the police interviewed the mysterious blonde woman who dined with him and left the scene. According to an article in the *New York Times*, "Her identity was not revealed until Wednesday [April 12, 1989] when Michael Chertoff, first assistant United States attorney for New Jersey, called her to the stand during the racketeering trial of Anthony Louis (Bobby) Manna of Jersey City, the reputed head of the Genovese crime family in New Jersey, and five associates."[7] Her name was Judy Galip, a model, whose fiancé had introduced her to Schiff in 1987. When the couple married later that year, Schiff gifted them an all-expenses-paid honeymoon at the Georgian Hotel. As a thank-you, Mrs. Galip and her husband had arranged to have Schiff over to their apartment for dinner, but at the last minute a relative of Mr. Galip died in Ohio and he had to go out of town. Mr. Galip then arranged for his wife to have dinner alone with Schiff. They settled on Italian food at Bravo Sergio.

Mrs. Galip testified that when she and Mr. Schiff entered the restaurant, he stopped to talk to two couples who were dining, while she walked ahead to their table. After the shooting, she saw the couples on the sidewalk outside the restaurant, and one of the men paid for a taxi to send her home. She recounted, "They told me I didn't see anything."[8]

The day after the murder, Mrs. Galip went to Ohio to meet her husband. It was decided that she should contact the police, and one week later she met with them. Her testimony was part of the evidence gathered (including wiretapping) against Bobby Manna and his associates that pinned them to the murder of Irwin Schiff.

Supposedly, Schiff was murdered because he was skimming money that belonged to the mob. It was believed that

---

7. Sullivan, "Tapes Tell How Schiff Was Murdered."
8. Sullivan, "Tapes Tell How Schiff Was Murdered."

Schiff had been an FBI informant. Boy, did my father know how to pick 'em!

Schiff's relationship with FICB did not end when he was removed as a partner. Prior to the murder, it was Domenic Rabuffo who did the dirty work at the bank for both himself and Schiff.

It was determined that Luis Electrical had over $2 million in outstanding loans from FICB. Roadworks had more than $5 million in loans and overdrafts from the bank. How did this happen? Well, Luis Electrical gifted bank president Tibi Horovitz a forty-two-foot cabin cruiser costing $242,817, and Roadworks gave Horovitz "the use of three luxury cars and the services of a personal chauffeur."[9]

Horovitz was arrested at his home in February 1988. Jack Graff, another principal in FICB, was also arrested on charges of laundering money for jewelry companies. The bank was a hotbed of corruption.

I had often wondered what happened to Rabuffo, having never seen nor heard from him after the bank drama. My father said that he didn't know. It wasn't until recently, when I began doing research for this book, that I learned the truth.

> Rabuffo had complained to his mob friends
> that Schiff, his long-time business asso-
> ciate, was talking about going to the feds
> and was "acting crazy." Following the mur-
> der, Rabuffo nervously sought out Herbert
> (Johnny) Novick, a 62-year-old alleged
> money man for reputed Genovese crime
> family underboss, Venero (Benny Eggs)
> Mangano.

9. Leonard Buder, "Bankers Held in Case Tied to Restaurant Slaying," *New York Times*, February 4, 1988.

"You're okay," Novick reportedly told him.

Rabuffo was concerned for his safety, said Assistant U.S. Attorney, Michael Chertoff, who convicted several Genovese mobsters of racketeering charges in connection with the homicide.

Rabuffo "realized he may have unwittingly caused Schiff's death and wanted to make sure wasn't also killed himself," said a law enforcement source.

But Novick's assurances apparently were not enough to make Rabuffo feel secure. He began cooperating with authorities shortly after the Schiff slaying. Rabuffo was later arrested and placed in the witness protection program. He provided the Feds with information detailing his and Schiff's schemes to defraud FICB and other financial institutions of $29 million in loans. Investigators found that Luis Electrical had made over $10 million in payments to Schiff, who authorities learned was a middleman between construction companies and the mob.[10]

Rabuffo seemed to have laid low for many years, but apparently, he did not appreciate the second chance that he had been given. One morning in 2014 I was reading the *Miami Herald* (I had moved to Miami in 2012), and there was an article on Domenic Rabuffo and his wife, Mae, who were both found guilty of a $49.6 million mortgage fraud scheme. Prior to their

---

10. Jerry Capeci, "Fat Man's Slaying Pushed Pal to Sing," *Daily News*, October 17, 1989.

arrest, the couple was living in the Ritz-Carlton in Coconut Grove, just blocks from where I live now.

Irwin Schiff and Domenic Rabuffo had been shining stars who burned brightly for a short while in my father's ever-changing night sky of friendships and business associates.

***

I left the bank at the end of December 1987. It was a freezing, late afternoon as I walked from Forty-Second and Fifth Avenue to Fifty-Fourth and Second Avenue, the whole time thinking about the mess of the past year and how I had only myself to blame for where I was in my life. I was going to make 1988 better. I had turned a corner as a result of the bank fiasco and the realization that my father made bad choices when it came to friends or, rather, just bad choices in general. I was resolved to find my next job on my own and to get as far away as possible from my dad's influence. *Sounds good, doesn't it? About time, isn't it?*

Despite my departure from the bank, I knew that more trouble was just around the corner.

CHAPTER 2

THE AFTERMATH

True to my resolution to find a new job that had no ties to my dad, I answered an ad in the *New York Times* and found a terrific position as a regional director for the Israel Tennis Centers, a nonprofit organization with an office in New York City. It was December 21, 1988, about 4:15 p.m. My boss was out of the country, and the bookkeeper and I were the only ones in the office, each doing our own end-of-day rituals. I phoned my mom at her home on Long Island. This was one of maybe five phone calls between us each day (an unhealthy codependency that persisted for most of my adult life). I wanted to tell her that I was leaving the office soon, and yes, the weather was unbearably cold, and yes, Mark and I would be staying at home that night.

I assumed that the knock at the door was our FedEx guy making his usual late-afternoon delivery, but I was wrong. It was a man and woman dressed in business clothes, flashing FBI badges and asking for me, just like they do on TV. My heart was banging, the fluorescent office lights seemed blinding, and a chill ran up and down my arms. I was experiencing the primal fight-or-flight reaction, but my body was frozen from head to toe. I remember trying to act normally, as if this visit was a routine appointment with a salesman. I led them into my office where the man handed me a subpoena. I asked them, with hands and lips trembling, to please explain what was happening.

The agents were not sympathetic to my panic, though I hoped at least the woman would be. There was no good cop/bad cop routine, only bad cop. It was very clear that they meant serious business. I pleaded, "Please, I don't understand. What is this about?"

"Get yourself an attorney," he coldly advised. "He'll explain it to you in detail. You are being summoned to appear as a witness before a grand jury in Brooklyn."

At the time, I didn't even understand what a grand jury did, but over the next couple of weeks, I got a crash course in the criminal justice system.

"Why?" I begged as the tears came. The fear was so powerful that I thought I would collapse. "What did I do? Can you please tell me what I did?"

"Your parents are leaving for Miami next week with Benny Mangano and his family. Tell them we said to have a good trip."

"How do you know that they're going? I don't understand! Can you please explain it to me?"

"We had a warrant to wiretap the phones at your parents' house," he said matter-of-factly.

"What? Why would you listen to all the conversations between me and my mom and dad? Why? Please!"

"Have a good night, Lisa, and get yourself an attorney."

I walked them to the door and called my mother immediately.

"Ma, FBI agents were just in my office. What's happening? Get in touch with Daddy. I have to talk to Daddy."

My mother didn't seem to share my panic. Perhaps she already knew what was going on, or perhaps all her years married to my father had hardened her to the pitfalls of the wiseguy lifestyle. It was also possible that she was just being the mother I knew, never particularly sympathetic. After all, she wasn't the one who had received the subpoena.

"I'll try to get ahold of him" was the best that she could do in the pre–cell phone era. "Go home, Lisa. I'll tell him to reach you there."

"No! He's gotta call me now! Ma, I can't go home until I speak to him! I won't make it to the subway! Ma, I feel like I am going to faint!"

I sat at my desk and waited for my dad to call. My mind reeled with thoughts about all the horrible times that I knew could be ahead.

My father finally called. He knew that several of his friends had been served with subpoenas earlier in the day. He never thought that I would get one; why would I? At least that was what he said to me. He told me not to worry, to go home, and to let Mark read the subpoena. He would call me later and tell me what to do.

I made it down to the subway and then to Grand Central Station, where Mark and I would take the commuter train to our new home in the river towns of Westchester County. I watched my fellow commuters search for their track and the train that would take them to their quiet suburban homes and their normal families. I wanted to trade places with any one of them.

I remember waiting to meet Mark by our designated track and thinking that nothing would ever be the same.

***

On Friday, December 23, 1988, two days after I received the subpoena to testify before the grand jury, my father arranged for us to meet with Mr. Hafetz, the criminal defense attorney whom he had hired to represent me. Ironically, that day was my parents' anniversary, and we normally would have been dining out as a family. Mr. Hafetz's office was near Grand Central Station, and I remember taking the subway from my office after work and meeting my father in front of the building. The streets were packed with tourists and suburbanites who were taking their kids into the city to view the Christmas tree at Rockefeller Center and the magically decorated store windows along Fifth Avenue. Office workers infused with the Christmas spirit were streaming out of their buildings en route to last-minute celebrations, shopping bags filled with gifts to give and gifts that were received. Mark and I were supposed to be going to our friend Andy Levine's thirtieth birthday party that night, but my appointment with my lawyer crushed our original plans. I could not believe that I was going to see a criminal lawyer. Me!

It became apparent that my father knew Mr. Hafetz quite well, a fact that unnerved me. Had he been my father's lawyer? Why would my father need a criminal defense lawyer? What was going on that I didn't know about? Was I part of a father-daughter team that needed representation?

My lawyer examined the subpoena, and the men discussed how it fit into the context of a known investigation that was underway involving my father's best friend, Venero "Benny Eggs" Mangano, the Genovese crime family boss under Vincent "the Chin" Gigante. Mr. Hafetz explained that I was being asked to testify about a few of my father's businesses that listed me as a corporate officer. Mr. Hafetz also explained the process of being a grand jury witness.

"I'm not allowed in the jury room with you, Lisa," he said. "Just answer all their questions truthfully and to the best of your knowledge. You shouldn't be in there long, maybe fifteen or twenty minutes."

***

On December 28, 1988, the heat in our bedroom went on at six a.m., signaling the start of the day. It was dreary and cold outside when Mark and I drove in silence to the courthouse in Brooklyn. I was terrified. I tried to tell myself that my fears were exaggerated, but I knew that they were perfectly justified. When I was not in a panic, I could intellectualize that none of this was about *me*! I hadn't done anything, but I had no idea what they wanted with my father. Would anything in my testimony hurt him? Would he go to jail? Would he go to jail because of something that I had said? What would my family do without him? Would this investigation go on indefinitely? Would I ever be happy again? These thoughts were circling around in my head, and I was at a loss to stop them. The only thing keeping me going was the reminder that I would be home in a couple of hours.

Mr. Hafetz was waiting for us in the lobby of the federal courthouse building. I remember how he and Mark talked and laughed about something and thinking how lucky they were not to be me. By the time we got upstairs to the courtroom, I was crying. The prosecutor introduced herself and called Mr. Hafetz and me into a private area where we could talk. She asked me if I knew why I was subpoenaed, and I answered, "Because my name was on my father's businesses." She told me that the investigation was not about me and that they just wanted information. I appreciated her effort to calm me down.

And then it was time to face the grand jury.

I sat down in the witness's chair. People were sitting on chairs in front of me. They were all a blur except for one older man. I turned my attention to him when I answered the questions because I could see that he understood how anguishing it all was for me. The questions went on and on, for almost two hours.

When they thanked me for my testimony and I left the courtroom, Mr. Hafetz and Mark were waiting for me. I told them as much as I could remember. I called my father on a pay phone to tell him that it was over. He and my mother were getting ready to leave for Miami the next day for a vacation with Benny and Louise Mangano and their family. I begged my parents not to go, that I was in a bad emotional state and needed them. My father told me that he had to go, claiming that they needed to show that they weren't afraid. My mother, always at odds with my father except for when it suited her, told me, "Daddy said we have to go."

I went home and got into bed for the next seven days.

My appearance in front of the grand jury had intensified my fears of what the future would hold. Worst-possible scenarios swirled around in my head, picking up strength as the days passed. I replayed the scene in court over and over, dissecting whatever I could, searching for signs that my father would be all right, and if he wasn't, at least it wouldn't be the result of something that I had said in my testimony. I couldn't eat, I couldn't get out of bed, and when I did sleep, I awoke soaked in sweat and in a desperate state of panic. My fear had taken over, and I wasn't rational anymore. My mother-in-law, Adrienne, with whom I was very close, babysat me during the day when Mark was at work. I was given the name of a psychiatrist at Beth Israel Medical Center in Manhattan, and he prescribed a new drug, Prozac, that was showing remarkable results with anxiety disorder. It took about two weeks for the medicine to do its work, and I gradually rejoined the world of the living.

My parents' departure to Miami when I was in that emotional state is something that I have tried to rationalize but have not yet been successful. They acted (and I am sure that they were acting) as if nothing out of the ordinary was happening! They phoned me daily, and I remember one of the calls going like this:

"How ya doing, Lisa?" my father asked, trying to sound cheerful.

"I'm not doing well, Daddy. I can't get out of bed, I can't eat, and I haven't gone to work. I'm having panic attacks."

"It's all going to be okay, Lisa. Listen to Daddy. Look, Benny is with me now. He's not worried, so why are you? Wait, I'm going to put him on the phone. Just a second."

"Daddy, please don't! I don't want to talk!" But he didn't hear. "Hi, Benny," I said nervously. "How is everyone?"

"We're all fine, Lisa. Lisa, don't worry about nothing. None of this concerns you."

I felt hysteria starting. "Thank you, Benny. Can I please speak to my mother?"

"Hi, Lisa, how are you?" Mother asked. She could not take hearing me cry; it was obviously too painful for her. She was suffering with me, in her own way. Unnerved, she babbled on, "We had a nice day today. The weather is beautiful. I walked around the Bal Harbour Shops, had lunch. We're going to Joe's Stone Crab tonight. What are you and Mark doing for dinner?"

* * *

Over the next several months, my anxiety had greatly lessened thanks to the medicine, some therapy, and the fact that nothing seemed to be happening with my father, until my parents and I received a subpoena. On April 3, 1989, we appeared at FBI headquarters in Lower Manhattan on a fittingly gray day to give handwriting samples. My father had put several businesses in my name, with my permission and my signature. When I was asked why he was doing so, he said, "This way you will have something when I die."

The new subpoena brought all my fears back to the surface. I remember that my mother and father not only didn't seem nervous about our situation but also appeared downright defiant and cocky. While my fear manifested itself as obsequiousness toward the federal agents, my parents let them know that they were not frightened. I wanted to be like them, but I was missing the bravery-in-the-face-of-the-FBI gene. In the waiting room, terror was reacquainting itself with my body, an ice-water feeling ran up and down my forearms, my mouth got dry and sticky, my breathing came quick and shallow, and my head felt too heavy to hold upright. I could almost feel the Prozac trying to fight the panic and save me, but it was no use. I went down in a crumpled, pathetic heap. I gratefully took a cup of water from the agent as she brought me into a room and told to me sign my name over and over again under her watchful eye . . . *Lisa E. Novick, Lisa Ellen Novick,* and *L. Novick.*

One year later, my father received notice from his lawyer that the investigation, as it concerned him, was over. By then, I had gotten my senses back and was able to resume my daily life. But the trauma of the last year had shaken loose all the pieces that had been hanging by a thread for a good part of my life. From the time the investigation started, when I was thirty years old, I've carried with me a bundle of raw nerves that even now, thirty years later, refuses to be controlled.

My father somehow turned the whole grand jury chapter into a life lesson. After he was cleared of any potential charges and I felt safe enough to talk about what had happened, I wanted to discuss my feelings with my parents as part of my healing. The results of my efforts were unbelievable, even by my family's standards! My mother told me, "Stop playing old tapes. It's over."

My father, well, this is the conversation that we had the first time I expressed myself on the subject:

"It was horrible for me, Daddy; the whole thing did a number on me. I was completely traumatized by the grand jury."

"Why? Nothing came of it," he said. "It was a fishing expedition. Nothing happened to you. Nothing happened to me.

What are you carrying on about?" He justified, "Besides, these things happen."

My sadness turned to anger then to fury. "Oh really? I don't know of anyone else who these things happen to! My friends have not gone in front of a grand jury! My involvement in this mess wasn't a random thing, Daddy. It happened to me because of *you*!"

"You want to be angry, be angry. You gotta grow up, Lisa."

What exactly was going on there? Was my father trying to teach me something? Because if he was, I didn't get it.

I knew that my father didn't really believe any of the nonsense rationale that he tried on me. I knew that he was terribly sorry for the pain that his reckless behavior had caused me. I knew how much he loved me. But I needed for him to take responsibility. The words needed to be spoken. But he just couldn't do it.

I still have bad dreams about getting letters to appear before an investigative panel. Even now, decades later, I get nervous when I open my mailbox and find a letter that I cannot readily identify or when a phone call shows up as "restricted." What horrible thing is going to happen next? My post-traumatic stress disorder was not solely caused by the grand jury experience; it was the culmination of a lifetime of anxiety-producing experiences.

How the hell did I get to this point? Truth be told, I always knew that someday something like this would happen. Just follow the bread crumbs.

CHAPTER 3

HERBERT NOVICK, MY DAD

Brownsville has always been one of Brooklyn's poorest neighborhoods. Even now, it has eluded the gentrification that has since made Brooklyn the hottest real estate borough among the five in New York City. Kids like me, who were born in Brooklyn and whose parents worked hard to move them out to the safe suburbs of Long Island and Westchester, now graduate college and plant their dreams and Ikea furniture in the once gritty neighborhoods of Williamsburg, Crown Heights, and Bushwick. Beginning in the 1880s through the 1950s, Brownsville was the home to many Jews who arrived from Russia. They lived alongside African Americans and Latinos who, by the 1930s, made up the majority of the community's population.

My grandfather Irving Novick was a sickly but gentle, kind man. When my father was fifteen years old, his dad suffered a heart attack that permanently ended his ability to work. He later developed Parkinson's disease and was totally reliant on my grandmother for his daily care. The family kept minimal possessions as they moved from apartment to apartment dodging the rent. My grandmother Frances was a hearty and stern woman who I am told was known as the neighborhood *farbissina* (Yiddish for "sourpuss"). She was always angry at someone. I remember her as a kind grandma who rarely smiled and was obviously very sad. I could see that she had little to be happy about.

As a young child, I reluctantly went to my grandparents' for sleepovers. An air of depression and hopelessness hung thick in the houses and apartments that they occupied, all devoid of photos, decorations, or anything that radiated warmth and permanency. It was as if they were camping in their homes rather than living in them.

There are just a handful of photos and even fewer stories from my father's childhood. My favorite is of a chubby-faced, smiling baby Herbert sitting up in his buggy. The next is a disturbing photo of the Novick family taken at his brother's Bar Mitzvah when Stanley was thirteen years old and my father was eighteen. By then my father was ruggedly handsome, tall, and solidly built, with thick, wavy dark hair. The most noticeable feature is that everyone is looking in different directions; no one is touching or smiling. There doesn't appear to be any connection between these four people! Strangers frozen forever in sepia. I have often thought how joyless the Novick home must have been and how desperate my father probably was to get away from them all.

Herbert had been a star player for the famous Thomas Jefferson High School Basketeers. I have a photo of my father at about seventeen years old shooting a basketball. There is something very sad about this photo as well; he is seemingly alone, with no other players and no people visible in the neighborhood beyond the gates of the playground. I imagine that the real-life scene was as colorless as the old photo. He had been recruited to play in a semipro basketball league, but that dream ended when he was forced to leave school and go to work to support his family once his father got ill.

In this respect, he was like many of the young men in his neighborhood who were cut off from professional careers due to a lack of money and education. My dad was street smart and very resourceful and took his responsibilities seriously. So, at seventeen years old, when several of the Italian men whom he knew from the neighborhood offered to introduce him to the powers that be at the Brooklyn dockyards, he gladly accepted. Known as a man's man, he had already earned a reputation as a leader with a tough, no-nonsense personality—someone who stuck by his word and could be trusted.

The dockyards of the New York City environs, which had been dominated by the Italians for decades, were a natural lure for organized crime. The vast array of cargo was easy to pilfer from as truck drivers who unloaded and loaded cargo were extorted. Their payoffs ensured that they would be selected to work. "At the shape-ups on the piers, where longshoremen would gather each morning in the hope of joining the group that would work on an arriving ship, it was common for a man to place a toothpick behind his ear, a signal that he would kick back some of his pay."[11]

The notorious Albert Anastasia, leader of the powerful International Longshoremen's Association and a close associate of mob bosses, hired my father. He was given one of the coveted "no-show" positions. Remember the episodes of *The Sopranos* where union leaders at constructions sites sat on folding beach chairs all day, reading the newspaper, watching TV, and sipping espressos? As a longshoreman, my father never had the pleasure of stepping foot on a ship. Instead, he spent many days hanging out with the guys in the Fulton Fish Market at Sweet's, New York City's oldest seafood restaurant.

11. Joseph Goldstein, "Along New York Harbor, 'On the Waterfront' Endures," *New York Times*, January 6, 2017.

Anastasia took a liking to my father, as did so many of the other waterfront bosses. Since the name Herbert didn't fit well with the Vinnys, Dominics, and Marios with whom he worked, his colleagues called him "John" or "Johnny." The name(s) stuck, even among the Miltons, Jeromes, and Seymours with whom he had grown up. Only his mother, with her thick Brooklyn accent, continued to call him "Hoybit."

Anastasia earned his ruthless reputation as the leader of Murder Inc., also known as the Brownsville Boys, a murder-for-hire business made up of Italians and Jews who operated out of a candy store in Brownsville. Throughout his "career," Anastasia was thought to have been responsible for murdering thousands of people. He later climbed the criminal ladder to become the boss of the Gambino crime family. He is perhaps best known for the way he was murdered. On October 25, 1957, while in his barber's chair at the Park Sheraton Hotel on Seventh Avenue and Fifty-Fifth Street in Manhattan, two gunmen assassinated him. His bodyguard had coincidentally left his post to park the car and go for a stroll when the assassination took place. No one was ever charged with Anastasia's murder, but there were plenty of suspects.

It was through Albert Anastasia that my dad met Funzi Tieri, who became the boss of the Genovese crime family in the late 1970s, and Benny Eggs. These connections ultimately shaped the direction of my father's life and influenced the choices he made as a future husband and father.

Writing this book made me desperately wish that I could go back in time and ask my father specific details about his life, especially what I had uncovered in my research. My father and I rarely talked about him, and now I understand why. For one, my dad was not a "sharer." He kept his feelings to himself. He also wasn't nostalgic; I don't think that the good old days existed for him. Perhaps most importantly, I never asked him questions; I think I knew that the answers were either too sad or too scary for me to process. What I later was told lived up to my concerns.

When my father was nineteen, he married a neighborhood girl named Selma, also known as Stormy. Her nickname alone was a portent of their doomed union. They had a son named Dennis, who looked just like his father and suffered greatly from his parents' tempestuous relationship. My father claimed that the marriage ended because Stormy "was a drunk." I suspect that my father's lack of attention to his wife and his son might have caused, if not contributed to, her alcoholism. After they divorced, Dennis lived with his mother, and our father would visit them on an irregular basis. I had heard that Stormy would leave Dennis alone at home at night for hours while she went out. Dennis developed a bad stutter at a young age, which he was never able to overcome.

My mother did not help the situation by refusing to allow Dennis to take part in our family life. As a child, I heard numerous heated arguments between my parents about Dennis. I never understood why my father allowed my mother to get her way on this issue. She had known from the start that he had a son. As Dennis got older, he despised my mother and was always angry at his father. I felt sorry for him and was ashamed that I was unable to help make his life better, but he could never have known that. He resented and ultimately hated me.

My father's brother, Stanley (hang on for this one), married his brother's ex-wife, Stormy, and thus became both uncle and stepfather to Dennis. A clear "fuck you" to my father. Their union was, not surprisingly, short-lived.

Stanley was a particularly sad product of the Novick home. He was tall and lanky, with very wavy, kinky, dark hair; pockmarked skin; and an argumentative personality. He also played on the basketball team at Jefferson High School, but unlike his brother, he got involved with many of the team members who smoked marijuana and used cocaine and heroin. Yes, these vices were a problem in schools even back then. Stanley eventually got hooked and ended up addicted to heroin for a good part of his life, bouncing in and out of jail for drug-related crimes.

In his twenties, Stanley took off to see the world and ended up on a kibbutz in Israel where he met a Jewish girl named Cathy from Argentina. They married, returned to New York in the mid-1960s, and moved into my grandparents' small house in Laurelton. They had a son named Raul, but Stanley's addiction, his inability to stay employed, and the cramped family quarters made it impossible to maintain any semblance of a family life. I found the screaming in the house unbearable to be around when my father would drop me off for visits. When Raul was still an infant and I was five years old, Cathy decided that she had had enough and packed up her son and took him to Argentina to be raised with her family. I remember being happy that she and Raul had escaped, thinking that nothing could ever grow in that house.

My father had tried to help Stanley get straightened out, but his assistance wasn't welcomed. Through his connections, he was able to get Stanley admitted into one of the most famous rehabilitation facilities of all time, the United States Narcotic Farm outside Lexington, Kentucky. The Farm, which opened in 1935, was a temporary home for many addicts dealing with drug-related demons. Many celebrities, particularly those in the record industry, had been residents. It was not until he was in his forties that Stanley, with the help of methadone, was able to control his addiction. He went on to become the administrator of Beth Israel Medical Center's methadone program.

Stanley's son, Raul, who eventually moved to Israel with his mother and stepfather, was raised with no connection to his biological father. His mother had told him that Stanley had died of an overdose (an honest mistake based on what she knew of his background) and that he had never tried to contact his son. When Raul was in his late teens, he began his search to try to find out what had become of his father. In the early 1990s, Raul, who was then in his late twenties and married, learned that Stanley was still alive and living in Brooklyn.

Although my father and Stanley hadn't spoken for decades, unable to overcome the terrible pain and anger that defined their joint past, my father and I were included in their reunion. There was no mistaking father and son, both strikingly similar in appearance and mannerisms. Late in life, after so many failed relationships, Stanley was catapulted into the dual roles of father and grandfather. They used their years together as best they could until Stanley died in 2007. Raul, who goes by the name Raul Novick, and I see each other whenever we are in each other's countries. We are first cousins who pat each other on the back and marvel at how well we have done despite the wacky Novick genes that we share.

I was left with an understanding of the horrors of drug abuse, a lesson that stayed with me throughout the peer-pressured years of experimentation.

CHAPTER 4

JANET MATLICK, MY MOTHER

My mother, Janet Lee Matlick, was born in Brooklyn to Frieda and Morris Matlick on February 16, 1933. My grandfather, one of nine children born in Russia, was a tall, thin, hardworking man. My grandmother, the oldest of two children, was sent to live with her aunt when her mother remarried and was unable to support her growing family. Frieda and Morris were very much in love throughout their marriage. Their lives were enclosed in a circle of respect, admiration, and devotion that seemed to those looking in (including their own children) complete and impenetrable.

My mother was distinguished from her peers by her exotic beauty. She was a Sophia Loren type with thick dark hair, olive skin, huge dark eyes, big lips, wide hips, and a full behind. Interestingly enough, she was never considered to be vain. While always well dressed and in full makeup, she was never an avid shopper for clothes or jewelry; she depended more on whatever my father brought home for her from his friends. Plastic surgery also wasn't a major concern. She taught me that people get old. That's what they do. Try to look the best for your age and *fartik*, or "finished" in Yiddish. Oozing sensuality without effort, she had the looks and strong-willed personality that perfectly suited her for the lifestyle she was to lead.

Though never clinically diagnosed, my mother has probably suffered her entire life from the mental illness known as borderline personality disorder (BPD). The *Diagnostic and Statistical Manual of Mental Disorders* lists nine symptoms for a BPD diagnosis, but exhibiting five or more of the behaviors is indicative of the illness.[12] She exhibited almost all of the symptoms in varying degrees: crippling fears of abandonment despite obnoxious behavior that pushed away those closest to her; sudden and drastic mood changes that were often unprovoked or inconsistent with the issues at hand; feelings of emptiness and hopelessness; intense anger that could last for hours or days and then disappear without resolution, as if nothing had happened; and dissociation, where she would stare into space, unable to process and deal with the anxiety and depression that plagued her. Individuals with BPD rarely seek help, believing instead that they are the victims of others' unstable behaviors. The illness affected every aspect of her life and ours as a family.

BPD is believed to be partially related to a mixture of genetics and childhood trauma. My maternal grandparents, who were extremely loving to me, may not have had enough time or skills to be the kind of parents that my mother needed. Janet Matlick spent a lot of time by herself as a child, out of both necessity and choice. Her parents worked long hours in the luncheonette that they owned down the block from the apartment, so she was left alone after school and for a good part of the weekends. Her sister, Lorraine, who was five years

---

12. Robert S. Biskin and Joel Paris, "Diagnosing Borderline Personality Disorder," *Canadian Medical Association Journal* 184, no. 16 (2012): 1789–94.

older and totally opposite in temperament, spent most of her time with friends.

To entertain herself, Janet spent a good deal of time reading. Her teachers, from kindergarten through high school, reported that she was exceptionally bright but fidgety and sulky. Not knowing how to handle such a "gifted" child, the teachers skipped their pupil ahead several terms. She never made it to graduation from Samuel J. Tilden High School; she walked out of the conference that her mother was called to attend at the guidance counselor's office. She did graduate from Boro Hall Academy at age sixteen.

***

Since Janet resented her parents' rigid work schedule that left them little time or energy to devote to her, she often punished them with stubborn, rebellious behavior. Some of the stories of Janet's iron will are amusing in retrospect, but at the time, her behavior was a major challenge for her family.

When she was six years old, the family took a summer weekend trip to a relative's farm near Hunter Mountain in the Catskills to relax and escape the city heat. When it came time to leave their apartment, Janet whined, "I don't want to go to the farm! I want to stay home!"

To which her mother impatiently replied, "Get in the car, Janet! You will have a very nice time at the farm. Papa says that there are lots of animals for you to play with."

When it was time for them to leave the farm on Sunday afternoon, my mother wailed, "I don't want to leave the farm! I am not leaving without my pet chicken!"

Unfortunately for the rest of the family, my mother had befriended a chicken, and they had been inseparable throughout the weekend.

"*Abruch*," my grandmother groaned (the word is Yiddish for "oh shit").

Anxious to get the show on the road, her parents gave in to the tantrum. Everyone, including the new barnyard pet, piled into the car for the long drive back to Brooklyn. Between the smell, the heat, and the chicken's flapping wings, the ride seemed endless. When they finally got back to the apartment, Janet's chicken was bedded down in the bathtub, and the cranky crew went to sleep.

When my mother returned from school the next day, the chicken was gone.

"Where is my chicken?" young Janet demanded.

My grandmother explained, "The chicken got very sick this morning, and Papa had to take it to the hospital."

My grandfather had given the chicken to the kosher butcher.

There was no peace in apartment 5D that evening.

When my mother was fifteen years old, she fell in love with a handsome Italian boy whom she had met at Tilden High School. When I asked her for details about the love affair, she initially said that it was too painful to discuss, but later opened up. My grandparents were furious with her for going with a guy who wasn't Jewish (even though they never practiced the religion) and made her life miserable when she refused to end it. She told me, "Daddy [my grandfather] had a temper. One day he was screaming at me about not seeing him anymore, and I got so angry that I ran into the bathroom and locked the door. When I refused to open it, he took a drill and removed the lock and then came at me with his belt strap."

"What did you do, Mom? What happened to you and the boy? What was his name? Did you ever think about him over the years?"

"Stop it, Lisa! Stop with the questions. I'm tired. I don't want to talk about this anymore."

My mother was seventeen years old when she started at the Katharine Gibbs School, where she met sixteen-year-old Junie Kaplan. Over lunches of tuna sandwiches and Dr. Brown's cream sodas at the Concord Cafeteria, Janet and Junie bonded over clothes, their similar strong-willed personalities, and their lack of seriousness in regard to their secretarial studies. The two young women, neither made of the toughest stuff, were known to have fainting spells on the subway ride to work during the sweltering, air-conditioning-less summers.

Junie introduced her new best friend to her fiancé, Herbie Silverstein, who thought that his brother, Marvin, and Janet would hit it off. After a short time, Marvin asked her to marry him, and she accepted, despite her concerns. She was not in love with him, but he treated her well and offered a way out of her parents' home and the drudgery of typing. Months before the wedding date, with the reality of the marriage setting in, she begged her parents to let her call it off. They refused, claiming that the plans were too far along.

My mother had a good indication that the marriage would be short-lived when she and Marvin arrived at the Glades Hotel in Miami Beach for their honeymoon. While Marvin was checking in to the hotel, my mother was flirting with the handsome valet attendant. Their holy matrimony was annulled soon after.

"Marvin was a very nice man," my mother told me over lunch one day when I was sixteen years old and she deemed me old enough to know that she had been married prior to marrying my dad. "He was like a brother to me. Or maybe like a father."

Junie and Herbie later divorced as well. They had two children, Syndee and Glen, who were called my cousins long before I ever understood our true connection. Junie died in December 2005. She was my mother's only close friend her entire life.

My parents' upbringings had many similarities. Neither celebrated much of anything—life achievements, birthdays, holidays, graduations, and so on. Neither practiced their Judaism. When I questioned my mother about this many years ago, she said that her parents and many others like them in the neighborhood chose not to observe; everyone wanted to be an American and leave behind the old country with its religious stigma, the poverty, and the pogroms.

One of the striking differences between my parents was the ways in which their childhood shaped their adulthood relationships to their parents. My father always helped care for my grandma Frances and grandpa Irving, both monetarily and by taking them to doctors, setting them up in new homes, going supermarket shopping for them, and so on. His involvement did not come easily; my grandmother's particularly difficult behavior usually resulted in my father getting disgusted and angry. When she developed dementia, my father scored a major coup by arranging for her to be accepted as a resident in the old, very prestigious, very hard-to-get-into Hebrew Home at Riverdale in New York. The setup did not last long. My grandmother's behavior was so belligerent and noncompliant that they asked my father to find another place for her to live. She was returned to the project-like apartment that she had previously occupied overlooking the boardwalk in the then desolate, crime-ridden Far Rockaway neighborhood of Queens of the 1970s and 1980s. I felt sorry for my father as he tried so hard to help her and to make her happy. It just wasn't to be.

Conversely, my mother never got beyond her childhood anger to want to care for her parents in their old age. I clearly remember horrible arguments between them while we lived in Brooklyn and later when we moved to the suburbs and they visited. I never understood how my mother could act so terribly toward them, even though I knew some of the background about their relationship. Before my grandpa Moishe died at home of colon cancer in his early nineties in 1983, my mother refused to go to visit him. No explanation given. When my grandma Frieda went into a nursing home in her late eighties, my mother also refused to visit. I never saw tears, though I won't say that she didn't shed them. My aunt Lorraine handled all death-related arrangements by herself. Though my aunt never asked for anything in return (she always had a kind understanding of my mother's limitations), my mother relinquished any inheritance to which she, or I or my sister might have been entitled.

CHAPTER 5

THE COURTSHIP OF JANET AND JOHNNY

Janet and Johnny met at a bar on February 23, 1956. He was taken by her beauty, and she was not taken by him at all. He was wearing a shabby suit, which he called his "rain suit," and from the way he put himself together, she had a feeling that he probably had a closet full of similar "rain" attire. He was vague about what he did for a living, and she knew right off that whatever he did do, it was not a typical desk job. She liked that he was self-assured and attentive and didn't play courting games. When they got together the next evening, he brought her a bottle of Arpege perfume. She told him that she had an ovarian cyst and would need surgery in the near future, and he told her that he would take care of her for the rest of her life. A Brooklyn-style marriage proposal.

Over the years, in flurries of opening up to me, my mother would describe her early years with my father. "He moved in with me on March 4, 1956," she said. "I was living by myself in a first-floor apartment at 455 Schenectady Avenue, downstairs from Grandma and Grandpa. He showed up with a paper shopping bag from Bohack's [a local supermarket] filled with his stuff, all his worldly possessions. And he kept his word, Lisa. He took care of me."

Janet and Johnny were very much alike in their strong, defiant, and perhaps deviant personalities. They had a connection to each other that even they probably didn't understand. My mother often said that their time together prior to marriage was the most wonderful time in her life.

My maternal grandparents did everything they could to discourage marriage between Janet and Johnny. Frieda would say, "Janet, he's too old for you! He has a son! Do you want to raise his son? What kind of job does he have that he goes to work at six p.m. and doesn't come home until eight a.m.? Is this the kind of life you want? Sure, he's nice-looking now, but soon he will be fat. Do you want to live with a fat man?"

Her last-ditch effort came one day as they watched from their fifth-floor apartment window as my father walked to his car.

"Janet, hurry, look at this, he has a bald spot on the top of his head! Do you know he has a bald spot? Today he has a spot, soon he will be completely bald! Is that what you want, a bald husband? A fat, bald husband with a child!"

When I asked my father about his first meeting with his in-laws-to-be, he had a slightly different take on how they felt about him. "They liked me," he said. "They were happy that I wanted to marry their daughter. In fact, Lisa, they warned me that she was sick and I would have a difficult life with her." My grandparents might have been referring to her problems with her cyst, or they were suggesting that she had some *issues*.

"But I didn't like them," he continued. "Your grandparents were very cheap people, never spent a dime! They wouldn't even pay for the wedding! They were relieved that I was taking their daughter off their hands."

Before she said "I do," Janet had a pretty good idea about the craziness she was marrying into. Her first meal with her soon-to-be in-laws, Frances and Irving Novick, was a Saturday lunch at their apartment. According to my mother, "It was like a circus! Everyone was talking loudly, and no one was listening. Your grandmother kept wiping everything with a filthy dishrag while she yelled, 'Hoybit! Hoybit! Come to the table. Come eat!' Your grandfather was propped up in a chair with a bib around his neck to catch the stray food that your grandma kept shoving into his mouth. He kept mumbling something, which I was sure was a warning to me to get out while I could. For dessert, she served Aunt Ida's famous dairy cake, which was wrapped in about ten layers of waxed paper to contain the grease."

These "romantic" courtship stories continued with Cousin Jakey's engagement party, which was the first time Janet met the extended Novick clan. The party, held at a Chinese restaurant in Syosset, Long Island, featured a simple, set menu for the guests. When my mother described the afternoon to me, she had a look on her face as if she were drinking a colonoscopy prep.

"Lisa, Daddy was always a pain in the ass. Such a troublemaker. He was never one to go along with rules. He wasn't happy with the limited meal choices that were offered, so he called the waiter over to do his own ordering. That's when chaos erupted!"

"Mmmmm, that sounds good," said Aunt Selma. "I'll have winter melon soup too . . . just like him." She pointed to my father.

"I'll have bird's nest soup," chimed in Uncle Jules.

"Hey, Johnny ordered spareribs," said Sareta. "I love spareribs! Give me an order of spareribs too."

"Make mine an order of roast pork," added a cousin.

The disgusted waiter eventually made an announcement:

"YOU HAVE A CHOICE OF WONTON OR EGG DROP SOUP! NO WINTER MELON SOUP! YOU HAVE A CHOICE OF EGGROLL OR SHRIMP ROLL! NO SPARERIBS! YOU HAVE A CHOICE OF CHOW MEIN OR EGG FOO YOUNG OR CHICKEN LO MEIN! NO SHRIMP WITH LOBSTER SAUCE! NO SPECIAL FRIED RICE! NO STEAK KEW!"

"I'd never seen anything like it, Lisa," my mother recounted. "They acted like they had never eaten before! I thought that Jakey was going to have a stroke. You could just see him adding up the bill in his head."

My mother says she is willing to bet that many years ago, in some shtetl in Minsk where my father's relatives came from, there was a big plaque over the door of the village insane asylum that read Welcome Novicks.

***

My parents were married on Sunday, December 23, 1956, at the Avenue R Temple in Queens. Since my father was notoriously late for all appointments (a habit that he was unable to control his entire life), my mother warned him, "Look, John, I'm telling you now. If you show up late for the wedding, there won't be a wedding! Do you understand?"

Much to my grandparents' dismay, Johnny arrived at the temple right on time. Janet and Johnny were a striking couple: she in a pink lace dress with a matching pillbox hat and he in a new dark-colored suit.

Following the ceremony, which was attended by only the most immediate family members, my mother and father got into a red-and-white DeSoto and set off to the small party at the Forest Hills Inn. My father shared the car with his friend Shimmy, the neighborhood shylock. Shimmy had a lovely wife, a son, and a Chihuahua named Pepe. (I was told that he also had another family with another woman. Apparently, things got a little heated at the cemetery when Shimmy died.) What Johnny didn't tell his bride until it was absolutely necessary was that the gearshift was broken and the car could only go forward. Uncle Max followed behind them in his car in case the ride to the restaurant involved any reverse driving!

It wasn't until the wedding was over that they settled into real life and got to know each other. Several days after the wedding, my father took my mother shopping on Belmont Avenue, home to all the Jewish food purveyors. He introduced his new wife to a friend who owned a wholesale seafood company.

"Hey, Johnny. Good ta see ya," the owner said as he slapped my father on the back. "And you must be the new bride? Congratulations to yiz both. I got a real beauty of a whitefish for ya today, John." The fishmonger referred to the fish in terms usually reserved for women rather than fins and gills.

During my parents' courtship, they had a very active social life, which included eating out almost nightly at restaurants in New York City. The whitefish would be the first real meal that my mother had made for her picky husband, and she was a bit nervous. That evening, she arranged his prized fish in a pan with potatoes and carrots and cooked it for the exact amount of time that he had carefully instructed.

"You should have seen your father's face," my mother told me. "He was so disappointed. How was I supposed to know that I had to cook the carrots and potatoes first? They were hard as rocks! I ruined his beautiful fish."

"So you know what your father did?" she continued. "He thanked me for trying, gave me a short lesson in parboiling, got up from the table, grabbed his leather jacket, kissed me on my head, and said, 'Gotta go, Janet. I own the crap game tonight. Don't wait up. Love you.'"

In reading FBI files from the 1960s, I learned that Funzi Tieri, the eventual capo of the Genovese family and my father's very close friend, made his reputation by running floating crap games and sports betting. My father was on his way up.

CHAPTER 6

LISA ELLEN NOVICK, THAT'S ME

I was born on May 20, 1958, at the Lutheran Hospital in Brooklyn to Janet and Herbert Novick. My birth certificate reads "Father's Occupation: Salesman, Mother's Occupation: Homemaker, Religion: Jewish." For the first six years of my life, we lived at 455 Schenectady Avenue in Crown Heights, on the fourth floor, in an apartment a flight below my maternal grandparents, Frieda and Morris.

My mother suffered from postpartum depression after I was born; mothering didn't come naturally or easily to her. She was unable to cope with nighttime feedings and diaper changes, so I slept at my grandparents' apartment. In the morning, I was returned to the care of my mother and the nanny. She jokes that my life was at risk whenever I was in her care and laughingly tells the story of my numerous brushes with death. *A real riot.*

"I'm not exactly sure how it happened," my mother told me. "I strapped you into your carriage. Remember your big blue carriage? Such a nice carriage. Well, I parked the carriage outside the deli on the corner of Lefferts Boulevard while I went inside to get a frankfurter and soda."

In those days, it was quite common for children to be left outside stores while parents ate or shopped. There was little risk of a child abduction, but a parent still needed to use a little common sense, or *sechel*, as it is known in Yiddish, when leaving a child unattended.

"I guess I didn't strap you in tight enough, because no sooner did I bite into my hot dog when a lady outside the deli started to scream for help. Everyone in the store ran outside, and there you were, Lisa, dangling upside down from the carriage, your little *keppe* [Yiddish for 'head'] only inches from the pavement."

***

Another near disaster occurred when my parents left me inside the car, in the heat of the summer, with the windows and doors closed (to ensure my safety), while they had lunch in a deli on Queens Boulevard. My mother described the scene when she and my father, thirty-five minutes later, finished their lunch: "When Daddy and I opened the car door, it was like an oven inside! Your little face was beet red, and your whole body was drenched in sweat. Daddy ran back into the deli and got cold towels to wipe you down. We were really scared, but you seemed okay after a while."

As if that wasn't enough, when I was four years old, my mother's friend Junie brought Glen and Syndee over to the apartment for lunch. The child-friendly menu consisted of bagels and whitefish. My mother teased Junie as she mushed up the whitefish chunks with her fingers in search of any bones before she fed it to the kids. I was not as lucky. My mother fed me the fish intact.

I almost emerged from the meal unscathed until there was a cough, then another, then a scratchy feeling in the back of the throat. My mother, panicking, rushed me over to the window (to get the best light), opened my mouth, and using pointy-edged tweezers (the best for plucking stray eyebrow hairs), tried to get out the one-inch whitefish bone that had lodged itself in my tonsil. She poked around as I cried and gagged and begged for her to stop. Junie could not help but say, several times, "I told you so!"

Luckily, my father came home and had the idea to call the dentist whose office was down the block. He easily dislodged the bone with one of his dental instruments, and I remember him holding it up in the light for us to see.

"Mrs. Novick," he said, "in the future, if you want to feed your daughter fish, I suggest you carefully search for and remove any bones. You got lucky this time."

My throat was all scratched up as a result of my mother's attempts to save me from a certain death. I drank up all her guilt-fed attention as she took me home and got me situated all comfy on the couch where I proceeded to take a long nap.

How many more times would I survive getting thrown back into the ring? It was amazing that I ever lived long enough to attend kindergarten! I made certain that as a parent I was a bit more attentive!

***

I spent most of my days in the company of Bernice Williams, or BC, as I called her. My beloved nanny had come north from Virginia years earlier to find work.

BC had coarse, messy hair that she always pinned up into a beehive, honey-colored skin, freckles around her nose, and a smile that flashed a couple of gold teeth. I loved those gold teeth. I wanted to have gold teeth too. She ate mayonnaise with everything and made clicking noises with her tongue as if she were always trying to get food out of hidden places in her mouth. She came to our home three times during the week to clean, care for me, and give my mother time for herself.

We kept to a pretty strict schedule, as did most of the nannies in the building, which I liked. Mornings were for cleaning, doing laundry in the communal washers and dryers in the apartment building's dark basement, and dancing to my records. Lunch was a grilled cheese, cream cheese and jelly, or tuna sandwich and Campbell's chicken noodle soup while the soap operas played on the TV in the den. After lunch we took a walk to the park. Only rain or snow kept us housebound. BC would dress me for the freezing cold or the sweltering heat, and would pack a survival bag with drinks, tissues, and a snack.

Along our route we usually stopped to pick up Harvey, a chubby blond-haired boy my age, who always smelled like Ivory soap. He made it very clear that he was in love with me, but I was not interested. Harvey's parents owned the pharmacy on the corner of their apartment building and worked every day. His nanny, Rowena, was BC's friend, so we spent a lot of time together. We would go to the nearby park when the weather permitted or play in Harvey's apartment.

CHAPTER 7

FROM BOZO TO THE QUEEN OF OUTER SPACE

Helicopter moms were not flying around Brooklyn or the rest of the United States, for that matter, in the 1960s. Children were expected to entertain themselves, and our neighborhood provided lots of opportunities to hone our creative skills.

Beginning at age five, kids were deemed old enough to play outdoors alone after dinner on either the front stoop of the building or in the back courtyard. Mothers periodically checked on their little ones from their apartment windows. The older kids were instructed to keep an eye on the younger ones. When the weather was good, we played hopscotch using colored chalk to draw the game's diagram on the sidewalk. We played hit the penny with soft, pink-colored Pennsy Pinky balls. We jumped rope to lyrical rhymes such as "I Like Coffee, I Like Tea," "George Washington Never Told a Lie," and "Teddy Bear, Teddy Bear." We folded paper into intricate panels to create fortune-tellers that fit over our fingertips and revealed the secrets to our future. We manipulated string into complex patterns known as rock the cradle, witch's hat, cat's whiskers, and Jacob's ladder. We determined our turn in a game's lineup via rock, paper, scissors; "One Potato, Two Potato"; and odds and evens. We kept very busy!

We snacked on candy such as Bonomo Turkish Taffy, Sugar Daddy lollipops, Jujubes, and candy necklaces, which easily helped us part with our stubborn baby teeth. We drank bright-colored sugar water from miniature soda bottles made from wax, we chomped on pastel-colored dots stuck on long strips of white paper, and we ate Peanut Chews and Mary Janes, having never heard of peanut allergies.

After school or on long summer days, we went to the local park, which was a child hive of activity, even in the winter. There were tall steel sliding ponds, monkey bars, swings for both babies and big kids, a sandbox, and wooden-planked seesaws that gave me splinters. There was no cushy foam or forgiving woodchips like they have today; if you fell off the equipment, you fell onto concrete and cracked your head open.

In the summer there was a fountain, and the kids would run in and out of the water while their nannies sat on benches on the sidelines with towels and encouragement. Around three o'clock every afternoon, the music from the approaching ice cream truck would send us running outside the park's black iron gates to line up to buy ice cream cones, bars, or sandwiches with handfuls of pennies, nickels, and dimes. We sat on the benches in nanny-child-nanny-child order and licked and bit our way through our treats. Our nannies' napkin-wielding brown hands wiped our sticky mouths and sent us back onto the playing field.

When cold or bad weather kept us indoors, we played in each other's apartments with Barbie dolls and G.I. Joes (the original playdates), practiced doing tricks with our Duncan

spinning tops, and learned to ride our bicycles without training wheels in the building's hallways.

***

When I wasn't involved in group activities, I would hunker
down on the green nubby fabric couch in the den and watch
television on our enormous RCA color set. I turned the big
dial and plunged myself into the world of cartoons, children's
shows, and movies inappropriate for my age such as the *Queen
of Outer Space*, *King Creole* with Elvis Presley, *The Eddie Cantor
Story*, and *Caged*. I loved channel 9's *Million Dollar Movie*
series because the featured movie was shown three times on
Sundays, and if a movie caught my fancy, I watched it every
time! My favorite was *The Minotaur: The Wild Beast of Crete*,
a 1960s Italian movie that was dubbed in English. During the
movie's opening dance scene, I would take a long scarf from
my mother's drawer; pin it to the top of my short, curly hair;
and, wearing my bloomers and undershirt, gyrate along with
the long-ponytailed Grecian slave girls doing their sacrificial
dance of the virgins. There was no parent to censor my choices;
as long as I was occupied, anything was a go. There were no
Baby Einstein CDs back then, and Barney, the big purple dino-
saur, was still extinct.

I spent lots of time listening to music on our console stereo
in the entry hall. I liked many of my parents' albums, including
Wayne Newton singing "Danke Schoen" and the Barry Sisters
singing songs in Yiddish. I had my own collection of 45s, and
I knew all the words to my favorite songs such as "Please Mr.
Postman," "Does Your Chewing Gum Lose Its Flavor (On the
Bedpost Overnight)?," "Norman," and "Take Good Care of My
Baby." I would dance the mashed potato and the twist, dances
that I had learned from watching *Shindig!* and *Hullabaloo*.
When I got the first Beatles album, I fell in love with Paul and

stopped listening to anything else. While doing my research for this book, I learned of my father's close contacts in the record industry, which explains why a four-year-old had such an extensive record collection.

My favorite pastime was to play house in the unfurnished living room of the apartment. I liked to pretend that I was a mom, dressed up in high-heeled mules, an apron, and white gloves. I carried a big leather pocketbook that housed an assortment of motherly possessions that included a set of keys, a brush, a tube of lipstick, and a pack of Viceroy cigarettes. I would pretend to cook and tend to the baby and chat on the telephone with a cigarette hanging from my lips. In case you're wondering, as an adult, I run my real house very differently!

When I wasn't busy playing, I was at school, P.S. 221 on Empire Boulevard, up the block from our apartment. The severe brick structure, which had been built in 1940, possessed all the welcome and warmth of a turn-of-the-century penitentiary in upstate New York, or an insane asylum in Victorian England! No wonder I had a nervous stomach each morning before school.

The windows in the classrooms were so high that the shades had to be opened and secured in place by a long pole with a hook on the end. The wooden desk and chairs were one unit, bolted to the floor in rows. The teacher's desk, always neat and sans personal effects, was centered in front of the blackboard. Her interaction with us was formal; she was our teacher, not our friend. There was no talking unless spoken to, and behavioral infractions were dealt with by a visit to the school office.

Our lessons were repetitive and geared to accommodate the needs of even the slowest student in the class. We practiced writing each letter of the alphabet over and over in our black-and-white marbled notebooks, both in the classroom and for homework. We went around the room reciting "One plus one equals two" and so forth until I was so bored that I struggled to stay awake. Tuesday was assembly day in the auditorium, and both boys and girls were required to wear button-down white shirts and navy pants or skirts. We stood to salute the American flag, and the music teacher played "God Bless America" on the piano as we stood and sang in unison.

CHAPTER 8

FATHER-DAUGHTER TIME

I have few memories of spending father-daughter time in my early years; he simply was not around very much. However, whatever time we did share was precious. He called me "Lisa Pizza."

Our one-on-one time involved watching television together on the couch, my head propped up on his big stomach. We watched movies that he chose, *Ben-Hur*, *A Night to Remember*, and the TV series *The Twilight Zone* and *Chiller Theater*. I was terrified by the latter, but my father would tell me that I had nothing to be afraid of, it was all fake, and I had to be a big girl. I didn't want to disappoint my father by being babyish, so I watched. I had nightmares that would wake me up in a panic.

Feeling terrified while watching scary shows marked the beginning of lifelong lessons about strength and courage that my father, tacitly or explicitly, tried to teach me. I never doubted that many of the painful lessons were well intended; he must have felt it crucial that his daughter learn to face life's challenges head-on, just as he had been forced to. However, I have

a big problem with his failure to recognize the inappropriate-
ness of many of the lessons for my age, my emotional state at
a given point in time, or my core personality. The raw content
and execution of his teachings, combined with the uncertainty
and ongoing stress of my homelife, resulted in my becoming a
very sensitive and extremely anxious child and adult.

On many occasions, I was my daddy's date at functions that
my mother did not want to attend. My mother would dress me
up in a beautiful little party dress with Mary Janes, and he and
I would go to a Bar Mitzvah, a Communion, or a wedding.

Invariably, my dad would leave me at the table with a relative or friend who would fawn over me, using a tone of voice
that I now reserve for talking to my cats.

"Oh, Lisa. Look how pretty you look. Seymour, look at
Johnny's daughter Lisa. Isn't she pretty? That dress is so pretty.
And those shoes are precious. What a pretty, well-behaved girl
you are. So big for your age too! Isn't she big, Sy? Where's your
mommy today? How come she's not here?"

"She had a headache. A very bad headache," I might say. Or
was it a bad cold? Maybe a bad cold that brought on a headache?

Most of my father-daughter memories revolve around
going along with my father on his "stops" or appointments to
meet his friends/business associates. Sort of a "kill two birds
with one stone" arrangement. I didn't care where we went; I
just wanted to be with him.

I remember going with my father on a Sunday afternoon
to see Frank "Funzi" Tieri, or "Uncle Funzi," at his home in
Brooklyn. It was the early 1960s, and the NYPD had then
described Funzi as the biggest loan shark in the country, having controlled most of the gambling and loan-sharking in the
Bronx, Brooklyn, Queens, and East Harlem. In 1972, after the
murder of acting boss Thomas Eboli, Funzi became the boss of
the Genovese crime family.

Funzi looked and acted like the old-time mafiosos who were depicted on TV. He dressed nicely, was very smart, and was either tough or charming as the need presented itself. Funzi had been married to a woman named America, but he also had a longtime mistress named Rita Berti, who was a famous opera singer in Napoli. Funzi had set her up in a house near him and his wife. Rita and my mother were good friends. I have the gold-and-diamond pin of a Great Dane that Rita gave to my mother as a gift when she returned from one of her trips to Italy.

Funzi told everyone that Johnny Novick was like a son to him and had to be treated accordingly. Had he not had so much respect for my father, he might have acted on his obsession with my beautiful mother. It was no secret that Funzi was in love with her, despite their large age difference. My mother told me a story that seemed to come right out of a mob movie. My father had to make a quick stop in Brooklyn with my mother one evening prior to them going out to dinner in Manhattan. My mother remembers being dressed in a beautiful red suit with a matching hat that sported a feather. They arrived at a storefront bakery that had a warehouse in the back. Funzi greeted my parents and told my father to stay in the bakery while he escorted my mother to a back room. Behind the door was a large table with about twenty men seated, who all promptly stood up when Funzi entered the room, holding my mother by the arm.

"This is Janet," he announced. "She is Johnny's wife, but she is my sister. She is always to be treated with respect. If she needs something, you are to make sure that she gets it."

My mother laughed when she recounted the story. "Funzi was always very vain," she said. "Lisa, there was no way that he could have brought himself to introduce me as his daughter!"

Funzi's behavior always remained appropriately fatherly or brotherly, and though my mother adored him as well, neither ever crossed the line.

I was fifty when I asked my father how he was connected to Funzi, aside from them being good friends. Prior, I had many suspicions over the years, but it didn't matter to me; I had no need to know. It was Funzi who was the silent partner behind my father's soft pretzel business known as New York Pretzel. You will hear details about the business a bit later. Funzi's daughter, Milly, worked in the office in the 1960s when it was on Boerum Street. The large, salty, doughy pretzels were baked in Williamsburg, Brooklyn, and trucked to kiosks in the subways, outside department stores such as Alexander's and E. J. Korvette, and to the ubiquitous street vendors whose iconic carts sold our pretzels along with hot dogs and soft drinks. Many a commuter, tourist, and office worker was saved from near starvation thanks to those deliciously twisted lumps of carbohydrates!

In the late 1970s and early 1980s, Funzi went in and out of the hospital for gallbladder issues and eventually for throat cancer. Only family and a select number of close friends were given permission to visit at those times. Larry Paladino, also known as "Fat Larry," was Funzi's godson. Paladino's father sat continuously on a chair across from the bed and kept watch over the visitors. My mother tells a story that once when she arrived, one of the nurses asked, "Are you another one of his women?" She just laughed. Funzi always gave her the best greeting he could, depending on how sick he was. He would take my mother's hand in his and kiss it. He would take my father's face in his hands and kiss him.

In January 1981 Funzi was the first mobster to be convicted under the Racketeer Influenced and Corrupt Organizations Act, also known as the RICO Act, and was sentenced to prison for ten years. He died of natural causes in March 1981 before entering prison. My father felt as if he had lost a father, the man who watched after him, loved him, and helped him earn a living.

* * *

It was through Funzi that my father met his almost-for-life best friend, Venero "Benny Eggs" Mangano. Benny and his wife, Louise, and their children had always been a part of my family's life. My earliest memory was going to Joey's first Communion party at a restaurant in New York when I was around four years old. Growing up, I rarely saw the Manganos except for an occasional holiday event, dinner, or a major life celebration. It wasn't until my twenties, when we would regularly go to Atlantic City, that I would spend time in their company. I had no idea the role Benny would play in my later life.

Sometimes I'd go with Dad alone or both of my parents to visit a couple named Jamesy and Francey Deleo. Jamesy was very handsome. By the time I was five years old, I had already developed an idea of the type of man that I liked; I was drawn to the look of Italian men with dark skin and dark hair— preferably slicked back. Confident, friendly men who were smart in the ways of the streets were for me!

His wife, Francey, had teased-up hair and frosted pink lipstick. When we visited them, there were always kids playing together in the street, and my father would tell me to join them while he went into the house. I was shy back then, particularly with other children, and preferred to sit quietly with the adults and listen to their conversation.

My parents told me that Francey was sad a lot because before she married Jamesy, she had a son named Gerald. When Gerald was a teenager, he was killed in a car accident while drag racing with friends on a part of the road where they were building the Long Island Expressway. The driver of the car that hit him eventually turned up . . . murdered.

Years later, I learned from my mother that Jamesy had been shot on the steps outside his girlfriend's home. He was on his way home from a night at the fights (boxing matches) with friends. The killer was never found.

Francey certainly did have a lot to be sad about.

We often went to visit Aunt Georgia and Uncle Leo at their home in Queens. Neither were my real relatives, but that was what I had been told to call them.

Leo was a tall, handsome, dark-skinned Italian man with gray and white hair. When I'd see him on holidays such as Christmas and Easter, he would always be wearing a suit with nice shoes and clear-polished fingernails. He even smelled handsome! I knew even then that he was the kind of man that I wanted to marry someday.

Georgia was tall and thin with dark skin; a small mole by her lip; a manly short haircut; and big, black, cat-eye glasses. She wore sexy outfits like the women wore on detective shows: tight pants that stopped at her calves, low-neck blouses, and high-heeled pointy-toed shoes without backs—as stylish today as they were in the early 1960s. Her bony, long-fingered, veiny hands, which ended with pointy red-painted nails, often held a cigarette holder or a drink. Mom told me that Aunt Georgia was Greek and was "a handsome woman." She had her own style, which included a big smile, a big voice, and a loud laugh as if her feelings just needed to bust out. I wanted to be just like her someday. I would sit quietly on the swivel chair in their living room and carefully watch Georgia's and Leo's every move. I loved the way she called him "daddy."

She'd say, "Daddy, can you get me another drink? Or "Daddy, can you turn up the music?" Or "Oh, daddy, you shouldn't have!" They were so in love with each other.

Their teenage girls dressed and acted like their celebrity counterparts on my favorite TV shows: *The Patty Duke Show*, *The Adventures of Ozzie and Harriet*, and *The Donna Reed Show*. They wore gold crosses around their necks and were respectful to their parents and helpful in the kitchen. I couldn't decide if I wanted to be them or their little sister. One night, after having dinner at their home, the girls asked if I could sleep over. I borrowed pajamas and slept in between them in a big bed. Uncle Leo made us breakfast in the morning. My father picked me up later that day.

The girls had an older brother named Chris. He was tall with black hair and was always nice to me. He was a soldier, and I remember he once came home when I was over at the house. He wore a khaki outfit, and I helped him unpack his big green duffel bag.

I learned later that Leo and Georgia were never married. When Leo died, two sets of wives and children showed up at the funeral. I guess that Georgia had wanted Leo's love so badly that she agreed to accept him on a part-time basis. The kids, who were theirs biologically, must have been told some story early on to explain why their dad was not home every day.

Chris later killed himself.

FBI records indicate that Funzi Tieri had been an undisclosed owner of Leo's businesses, Frigid Express Inc. and the Pecora Trucking Company.[13]

I could never get enough time with my father my entire life. I knew how much he loved me. I also knew that he was either unwilling or unable to give me the attention that I always craved.

Sometimes my mother left me alone in my father's care. It didn't always end well. One snowy evening my father talking on the phone in the kitchen woke me up.

---

13. Federal Bureau of Investigation, field office file NY 92-2476.

"Where's Mommy?" I asked my father as I entered the kitchen, where I found him eating a sandwich.

"She went to play cards at a friend's house. She'll be home soon. Why don't you go back to bed?"

I waited patiently for her return, assessed the weather conditions from my bedroom window, and started to panic when she didn't come home promptly.

"Daddy! Daaaaadddddy! Call Mommy and tell her to come home right now. I'm scared. It's snowing outside, and it's dangerous for her to drive."

After numerous attempts to calm me down, he finally picked up the phone. As I stood over him to make sure that he wasn't trying to fool me, he said, "Janet, Lisa won't stop crying. She wants you to come home. I think you better come home now."

"Look, Johnny, I just got here," I heard her annoyed voice say. "Put her back in bed and tell her that I am fine. Handle things, Johnny. I'm home every night with her."

I was put back in bed, and my anxiety got worse and worse. My four-year-old self was certain that my mommy would get into a car crash while driving home in the snow. I could see it all happening in my mind; she would die, and I would be all alone. I had my father call her again, only this time I took matters into my own hands.

"Mommy," I pleaded, "please come home right now. I'm so scared. Please come home."

Was I really scared, or just manipulative? Both, I think.

She didn't come home until she was ready. I cried until she walked into my room and I could see that she was okay. She was angry, but I didn't care.

The radiator in the hall made its clinking sound and filled our apartment with warmth. I looked out my window and saw that the snow had covered all the benches and trees and the tops of the Mister Softee ice cream trucks that were parked in the lot next to our building. I crawled back into my bed, surrounded by all my toys and dolls. My mother was safe at home. We were all safe. She wouldn't still be angry in the morning.

One morning my mother went out and left me in my room playing with my favorite doll, named Bunchie. My father was in the kitchen, glued to the telephone. I kept asking him to come into my room to get a toy for me that was on top of my dresser, but he would gently remind me that he had phone calls to make and would be in as soon as he could. Feeling rejected and pissed off, I decided to take matters into my own hands, copying a trick that I had seen a kid do on TV. I opened the bottom drawers of my animal-painted dresser and started to climb them, hoping to reach the toy. Not surprisingly, the dresser toppled over with a loud crash and fell on top of me. Oddly enough, I wasn't seriously hurt, and my father, so involved in his conversation, never came into the room to see what had happened!

"Daddy! Daddy, come in. Hurry! The dresser fell on me. Daddy, I am stuck. Daddy, I can't move. Come in now! Daaaaaaaadddddddy!"

I didn't feel hurt other than a few cuts and bruises, so when I got no reply from my father, I managed to free myself from underneath the drawers and stood up. I stomped into the kitchen and gave my babysitter a piece of my mind.

"Why didn't you come? The dresser fell on me! I was calling for you! Daddy, why didn't you come?"

He sized up my body parts quickly to see that everything was still located where it was supposed to be and, with the phone still cradled between his shoulder and ear, said, "Are you okay? You look okay. I'll be off in a minute, and I'll come in to see you."

If "you must be kidding me" had been an expression used back then by a kid, I am certain that I would have expressed it. But having not yet mastered the art of sarcasm, I slunk back into my room and had, what seemed to me at the time, a brilliant idea. To reenact the helplessness and pain that I had endured, I repositioned myself back underneath the fallen drawers and waited for my father to come in to save me. I waited and waited. Finally, my mother came home.

My father's lack of paternal instinct was evident early on in our relationship. It should not have come as a shock to me that many years later, when the stakes were so much higher, he never came to my rescue.

***

Time alone with my mother was also limited and precious.

My father bought my mother her first car for $25 from the gas station attendant who worked around the corner from Max's Deli on Sutter Avenue and East Ninety-Eighth Street. It was a light-blue Ford with straw mats on the front seat to hide the cracked and peeling vinyl. She put a thick blanket and a pillow in the back seat for my naps, and to protect me from the metal springs that poked through the ripped bench seat. I sat next to her in the front seat, no seat belts necessary (*Did the cars even have seat belts in those days?*), and we played the radio and sang along. When we would stop at a red light, she would make the car dance by gently stepping on and off the brake to the beat of the music.

The car gave us our freedom and time together. We would drive to Max's for lunch and eat juicy hot dogs and salami sandwiches on club bread with a side order of giant, oily, crinkle-cut french fries. Lunches were often followed by trips to the library. I was deposited in the children's book section while my mother perused the adult section. I would take home several plastic-covered books that I looked at over and over. Once a week we went to the beauty parlor on Utica Avenue, where I kept myself busy playing with the colorful bottles of nail polish at the manicurist's table. We would go to the Prospect Park Zoo, with its animal houses placed along tree-lined, winding pathways dotted with food and souvenir vendors, and to the big bank on Flatbush Avenue that had a giant replica of the painting of *The First Thanksgiving 1621* by Jean Leon Gerome Ferris. The scene of the pilgrims and the Indians preparing for the feast was so clearly imprinted in my mind that fifty-five years later I was able to visualize it and research its background.

We also spent a lot of time with Junie, Syndee, and Glen, or Glenny-Boy, as we affectionately called him. Sometimes we would take a full-day excursion out to Green Acres Mall on Long Island or to Manhattan Beach, but most of the time we would just visit their apartment and keep ourselves amused. Our mothers would sit at the kitchen table smoking packs of cigarettes and drinking endless cups of coffee. In the winter, we would stay inside and play monster or house or war. In the summer, we would stay outside and play monster or house or war or jump rope or hit the penny or go to the park across the street. Junie's father, Papa Benny, owned a dry cleaning store around the corner from their house. Our moms would often leave us playing in the cramped store, or we would sit at our kids-only table at the luncheonette while they had coffee at another table. These were happy childhood memories for me. Soft and safe.

CHAPTER 9

FAMILY TIME AT ITS BEST AND WORST

Our family time together ranged from magical to disastrous.

My parents fought constantly in my presence and were not shy to perform in front of the public as well. What were they always arguing about? The lack of money? How each envisioned our future? The limited time my father spent at home? Who knows? I was little. All I could see were two very unhappy people who seemed to hate being in each other's company.

On a cold, very bright, sunny afternoon, my mommy and daddy and I walked hand in hand onto the Staten Island Ferry. Still exhausted from the night before, I was happy though, relieved that the worst was over. I knew that this special outing was payback for what they had put me through, their earnest but naive attempt to pretend that all was and would be fine between them and us.

It happened on a Sunday evening. I remember because *Walt Disney's Wonderful World of Color* was on TV. My dad had spent the afternoon with his son, Dennis, and then brought him back to the apartment to have dinner with my mother and me. We never ate together, and I knew that nothing good was ahead when my father walked in, unannounced, with Dennis. My mother was furious, and she and my father were in the kitchen screaming. Dennis was in the den with me, and we were trying to watch TV and not listen to the increasingly horrible words going back and forth in the other room.

When I couldn't stand the cursing any longer, I ran into the kitchen and saw my mother hitting my father as he tried to get away from her. When she took her fist and hit him in the face, he pushed her, and she hit her forehead against the frame of the kitchen door. I can still hear the sound it made. She fell on the floor, and within minutes a very big, egg-shaped bump started to grow on her forehead. My father and I were terrified, thinking that she was dead. He wrapped ice in a dish towel and put it on her head. She was lying on the floor and whimpering, and I lay next to her holding her hand.

With all the screaming coming from our apartment, a neighbor called the police. The police wanted to take her to the hospital, but she said no, she'd go to the doctor the next day. They helped her into a chair and left. My grandparents came downstairs to take me up to their apartment to sleep. My father drove Dennis home.

The next day my mother and father were all back together as if nothing had happened. We all went to a doctor for tests to make sure that her brain wasn't hurt. Then they had a special treat for me . . . a ride on the Staten Island Ferry. I had become used to their guilt gifts.

We also visited Freedomland in the Bronx, which was on the site where Co-op City was later built. I have photos of our day exploring the entertainment park. I had been frightened on one of the darker amusement rides, and my father once again reminded me that it was all make-believe and that I shouldn't be scared. But I was. My parents had an explosive argument late in the day while I joined hands with a bunch of kids and square danced and did the hokey pokey. Everyone was looking at them fighting, which embarrassed and frightened me. There were lots of those types of days.

The Jade Cockatoo, a high-end Chinese restaurant in Greenwich Village, was one of my favorite places to go with my parents when I was very young. A tall, slim, white-haired Chinese man who was always dressed in a suit would warmly greet us and lead us into the dimly lit dining room. Gold, fire-breathing dragons peered down at us from red walls. The tables were covered with white cloths and were spread far apart for privacy. There were rarely any kids in the restaurant, only nicely dressed adults who drank cocktails from tall glasses and leaned into one another to talk.

Connected to the main dining area was a room used for banquets. The walls were covered with antique Chinese musical instruments and paintings of ancient Chinese landscapes with soft-pink and green trees, little bridges going over tiny ponds, and rickshaws being pulled by bent-over black scribbles. Glass display cabinets held assorted decorative objects including hand-painted porcelain spoons that had deep oval bowls in them like the ones we used for our wonton soup, beautifully carved enameled chopsticks that were used only for festivals, delicately painted hand fans, and colorful carved masks that were particularly scary when I could hear my parents' loud voices coming from the dining room. I would stay in the empty banquet room until I couldn't hear them fighting anymore, and I would think, *Aren't they ashamed to be fighting so that everybody can hear them? Don't they know how embarrassed I am by their bad behavior? How come nobody ever tells them to be quiet?*

Did I do something? Maybe they just don't want to be with me?

***

The car rides of my childhood years were when I witnessed some of my parents' most explosive arguments. Maybe it was the confined space of the car, or a previous disagreement that had spilled over from the apartment into the car, or the sports radio station reporting a "loser" for my father.

One evening we were driving in the rain to Bamonte's Restaurant in Greenpoint, Brooklyn. I was sitting on my mother's lap in the passenger seat while my father drove. The rain was coming down hard, and the windshield wipers on the Cadillac were working at top speed. To pass the time, my mother was telling me make-believe "Little Herbie" stories that featured my father as the fattest kid in the neighborhood who was bullied by all the kids.

"You see," my mother said, "Little Herbie was too fat to fit through the door at school, so he had to be hoisted up through the classroom window. Remember that day when you saw the piano being lifted up through the apartment window? Just like that!"

I pictured Little Herbie as a child-sized version of my daddy. He didn't look upset by the cruel stories, but I knew that they must have been very hurtful to him. I laughed anyway; my mother gave me the green light to be mean. I watched her give him self-satisfied looks. They liked to use me that way to get at each other.

When the story ended, I watched my mother take her finger and write "FUCK YOU" on the fogged-up windshield. I made a mental note to report everything to my grandmother in the morning.

* * *

The good times? They are my treasures, so precious that I can still see them. When the 1964 World's Fair came to Flushing, New York, we were regulars. We spent long afternoons into evenings touring the pavilions and eating everything from delicious Belgian waffle ice cream sandwiches to meals at the floating Cathay Restaurant in the Hong Kong Pavilion. Eating was the center of all our outings, which accounts for the major role it still plays in my life. My parents bought me a turquoise-blue felt hat with a pink feather that stuck out of the side where my name had been embroidered.

Walking back to our car one evening, my mother started to complain that her feet were killing her and she needed to rest for a few minutes. My father and I watched as she sat down on one of the numerous mushroom-top-shaped lights that surrounded the parking lot. It was clear to my father and me that these lights were strictly functional; they were not intended to be used as stools. We watched as she and the light crashed down, pocketbook and hat flying, legs up in the air. And we laughed and laughed even before we knew if she had gotten hurt. That was the way we did things in my family.

One summer night we went to visit Tony Lunch and his wife at their tiny bungalow in Far Rockaway. It was a wooden shack with almost no furniture, just lots of sand on the floor inside. They had just finished their dinner in the kitchen (we had gone to a restaurant), and the room was hot and still. There were no kids, so I sat by myself on the rocking chair on the porch and waited for my father and mother to finish talking. The ocean was right outside their door, the waves made a nice sound, and there were hundreds of stars; I could have sat there all night.

In June 1964, at my own insistence, I went for the full eight weeks to Kutsher's Camp Anawana, a coed sleepaway summer camp in the Catskill Mountains. The cost was an exorbitant $700, but my father managed to get the money. Months earlier, my grandma Frieda and grandpa Moishe took me to Kutsher's Hotel for the Passover holiday. I latched onto my counselor for the week, Leslie Landsman, who told me that she would be working at Anawana that summer. I wanted in!

I did remarkably well for a kid who had just turned six—so well that I continued as a camper for nine years! I was thrilled to be with my parents on visiting day. They made every effort to make the day special, and I can still remember a feeling of gratitude that they had restrained themselves from fighting. I have photos of me in my camp uniform, a bit chubby, with thick, bushy dark hair cut in an abbreviated Cleopatra style. Old black-and-white Kodak photographs show the Novick family at the waterfront and the basketball and tennis courts. I was the center of their attention; my brilliant smile says it all.

One of my happiest memories involved a local Chinese restaurant (I seem to associate food with joy) that we often visited, which catered to the Sunday night Jewish Chinese-food-eating crowd. Following a drama-free meal, I went to the front of the restaurant to keep myself busy while my parents sat at the table drinking tea and talking. It was just after Christmas, and a small silvery-white Christmas tree decorated with pastel-colored ornaments and white lights remained on display. I sat on a ledge by the cold window and watched the snow fall, the flakes dancing in front of the streetlights as they made their way down to the sidewalk.

On our short car drive home, "If I Had a Hammer" by Peter, Paul, and Mary came on the radio. I sat in the back seat and, for the first time, sang along with the radio in front of my parents.

I was always too embarrassed to sing or dance in front of my parents; I wasn't accustomed to their undivided attention, and they weren't the type to make a fuss and ooh and aah over their child. But that night in the warm car, with the windshield wipers thumping to keep pace with the snowfall, we were different people. That's magic.

CHAPTER 10

LAMB CHOPS AND LOVE

By this time, you are surely thinking, *This poor kid must have turned out to be a real nutjob!* Well, I certainly have my issues, but thank goodness there were many stable, caring people throughout my life. I was instinctively attracted to them, and they tempered the more painful times and helped fill in the missing pieces. My maternal grandparents were the ones who gave me the love, stability, and comfort that likely made the difference between my life turning out fairly normal or taking a very dark turn.

I spent at least one night each weekend sleeping in their apartment, one floor up from ours, and I would visit every evening after dinner for dessert and a good-night kiss. My grandma colored in coloring books with me, taught me to crochet, filled in numerous Venus Paradise color-by-number pictures, and let me go through her chest of drawers to find treasures and play dress up with her jewelry, pocketbooks, mink stole, and high heels.

She made me my favorite dishes, such as baby lamb chops and elbow macaroni with tomato sauce. There was always a bottle of Canada Dry ginger ale on the dinner table, which she quickly whisked away to be refrigerated after each glass was filled, as if the soda would spoil from sitting out on the table. Dessert, which was served no sooner than an hour after dinner to ensure the food had time to settle in our stomachs, was either cake from the famous Ebinger's Bakery or a dish of Breyers vanilla bean ice cream topped with a spoonful of strawberry preserves. Breakfast was orange juice that I squeezed by myself and pancakes swimming in Vermont maple syrup.

**

After we moved to the suburbs, my grandmother would come to help my mother. She arrived most Saturday afternoons on the Long Island Railroad with shopping bags full of Jewish-style delicacies like chicken soup and *knaidlach* (matzoh balls) and calf's liver, all reddish brown and slimy, which she would panfry with sautéed onions. Heavenly. Even the repulsive-looking raw cow's tongue, with its bumps and veins, would be turned into a delicious dish. I couldn't wait for her arrival each week. She never prevented my parents from arguing, but her presence comforted me. When she babysat in the evening, the house was blissfully quiet as we watched *The Lawrence Welk Show* and *Saturday Night at the Movies*.

Beyond my grandparents' apartment, there were lunches at Lundy's Restaurant in Sheepshead Bay, ice cream sundaes at Schrafft's, and cream cheese and date-nut bread sandwiches at Chock Full o' Nuts. My grandmother took me to see my first Broadway show, *Fiddler on the Roof* with Harry Goz, and my first concert, Lou Rawls, at the Brooklyn Academy of Music. She was also my only connection to an extended family. We regularly visited my great-grandmothers Tilly and Mary and attended many of the Matlick family gatherings, where I spent time with my numerous aunts, uncles, and cousins.

We also took long walks down Utica Avenue regardless of the weather. We did her shopping at the butcher with its big meat grinder on the counter and sawdust on the floor, as well as at the produce store, which had baskets of colorful fruits and vegetables that I could put into a bag and weigh. On these walks, which went as far up as Eastern Parkway, I would often ask her about the men who I now know were part of a Hasidic Jewish community known as the Lubavitchers. She told me that they were Jewish people and that I was Jewish too.

I knew nothing about my Jewish background; I had never heard of Passover, Rosh Hashanah, or Hanukkah, and I never entered a synagogue until years later when we moved to Long Island.

I was curious about the decorated little straw houses that appeared on their apartment balconies or in their backyards each year just as the leaves on the trees along Eastern Parkway began to turn beautiful colors. Delicious smells came from these huts at lunchtime, and I could hear children singing songs in a different language. My grandma told me that the little houses were called succahs and that the holiday was called Succoth. I thought how lucky the kids were to eat and sometimes sleep in these cozy huts, surrounded by their family and friends.

"But, Grandma, if they're Jewish, and we're Jewish, why don't we dress like them or celebrate Succoth like them?" I asked.

"They are very religious Jewish people," she said.

But I wasn't getting it. If we were the same, how could we be so different?

I equally adored my quiet, very kind grandpa Moishe. He and his brothers owned the coffee shop in the Pierrepont Hotel in Brooklyn Heights. He would leave for work at three a.m., six days a week, and I never heard a complaint from him. My grandmother got up with him every one of those days to see that he was dressed properly for the weather and to kiss him goodbye.

Grandma Frieda would take me to visit him at work, where I would sit proudly at the counter drinking a malted he made especially for me. The highlight of my visit was going to one of the rooms on the top floor of the hotel or for a walk on the promenade, where I looked out across the East River to see the Empire State Building and Chrysler Building glittering in the sunlight.

***

Sometimes after dinner my grandpa would sit in his overstuffed chair with me on his lap and sing. One song was from Russia, which began with words that sounded like "Saleka baleka" and ended with my grandpa gently spitting into the palm of my hand and saying, "Phooey!" Probably had something to do with warding off evil spirits.

He also taught me a song with a hypnotic melody that mimicked rocking back and forth on a seesaw. It went like this:

> *Seesaw,*
> *Margery Daw,*
> *Who's there?*
> *Grandpa.*
> *What do you want?*
> *A bottle of beer.*
> *Where's your money?*
> *In my pocket.*
> *Where's your pocket?*
> *In my pants.*
> *Where's your pants?*

I left them home.
Get out of here, you dirty old man!

In my later years, I got to thinking about the words and was horrified! I had to check it out with my mother to make sure that I hadn't made up the whole thing, but lo and behold, this nasty little child's song did exist! You can't make this stuff up!

CHAPTER 11

I HAVE A SISTER

I begged my parents for a sibling. My sister was conceived after a night of drinking champagne at the Copacabana. She was born on October 2, 1963. My mother's postpartum depression was even worse than the first go-around with me, and she was unable to care for my sister on any level.

We had a crib and a changing table set up in what should have been our living room, but they were rarely used. During the day my sister would be with my mother or BC for several hours, and at night she would sleep upstairs at my grandparents' apartment. On Saturday nights I would sleep upstairs as well. During the nighttime feeding and diaper changing, my grandmother would turn on the lamp beside my bed and cover it with a towel so that the light was soft and soothing. She cared for my sister when she was sick and for nearly one full year after we moved from Brooklyn to our new house on Long Island.

Arguments between my parents were constant then. I will never know why; my mother would never discuss it. I think that it was all too much for her fragile self to handle. One kid was barely manageable; two seemed impossible. My father's absence every evening and on the weekends must have also been difficult for her. Even if he was at home, he was not a hands-on father, nor was he supportive of her efforts to deal with her depression. The whole thing was a hot mess!

One evening I was carrying a carousel-like holder of newly cleaned glass baby bottles from my grandparents' apartment to ours when I heard my mother and father screaming from inside our apartment. I was shaking so hard that the bottles fell out of my hands and glass pieces spread all over the terrazzo floor of the hallway. My grandmother came down to clean up the mess and take me back to her apartment for the night. I cried myself to sleep.

My sister and my mother never bonded; they were at odds with each other from the start. They often had physical fights, and the police had to be called on more than one occasion. My mother and father could not agree on anything, least of all how to deal with my sister's issues. My mother tried to get her into therapy, but my father thwarted any attempts, claiming that there was nothing wrong with my sister.

"She doesn't need the help, Janet. YOU do!"

"Johnny, you are ruining this child! Don't you see what's going on here? No, you don't. You don't want to see anything," she responded.

My father felt enormous guilt over his role in both his son's and younger daughter's unhappiness but didn't take the steps to get them the medical help they needed. The lack of parenting and overall dysfunction in our home cost my sister, a member of Mensa, a chance to lead a normal life. My father spared no expense on schooling or apartments for her, eternally hopeful that things would get better, but they never did. There was just too much trauma for her to overcome.

Sadly, it has been fifteen years since I have seen my sister. For my mother, it has been more than twenty-five years. I have chosen to respect her privacy and not write about her in detail. The issues are far too complicated and deeply painful.

CHAPTER 12

LIFE IN SUBURBIA: THE EARLY YEARS

By 1965 the demographics of Crown Heights had changed. The predominantly white, Jewish populations moved en masse to the suburbs as African Americans from down south and the Caribbean islands moved in. My mother, who has never been good with change, refused to move at first; she would have stayed in the apartment on Schenectady Avenue forever had my father not insisted. She reluctantly participated in the search for a community to move to. My parents' arguments intensified over the monetary concerns of buying a house, the pressures of a move with children, and my mother's fears of being uprooted from the neighborhood she had known her entire life. They eventually agreed to build a home in the Five Towns (Hewlett, Woodmere, Lawrence, Inwood, and Cedarhurst) in Nassau County, Long Island.

One week prior to our scheduled move in May 1965, when I was just a few weeks shy of my seventh birthday, an incident at the Schenectady Avenue apartment building instantly changed the way my mother felt toward the impending move.

I was in the backyard playing with the neighborhood kids after dinner when everyone started running and screaming. I didn't know what was happening, but I took off toward the basement with the group. We ran into the elevator, and as the door was opening, a man was running toward us, cursing and telling us what he was going to do to us when we were caught. The door opened just in time, and we were able to cram ourselves in and press the up buttons before anything happened. When I arrived at my apartment, crying, my mother said, "What happened? Lisa, calm down and tell me what happened. Where is your other shoe—you only have one shoe on?"

"I was running with the kids. A man was chasing us. We were all scared, but we got away in time."

Then and there my mother decided that I would stick by her side until we climbed into the car to head eastward. I would not be going back to school for my last week at P.S. 221, and I would not be playing outside anymore. I was delighted.

For the Jews whose parents came from predominantly Eastern European backgrounds and who were raised in Brooklyn, Long Island was the Holy Land, safety from the urban turmoil that was bubbling over across the nation. There were beautiful homes with backyards and sodded green lawns, great public schools, synagogues, shopping malls, and an abundance of delis and Chinese restaurants. The Jewish American dream.

We made several Sunday trips to see all five of the towns, and my parents ultimately decided on a community in North Woodmere, which was being built on top of the Valley Stream dump. They chose a colonial-style home with a price tag of $37,000—a small fortune. My father had no idea how he was going to pay for the new house. He was never a saver; he was a gambler, and they are not mutually exclusive. Throughout our lives, there were no funds set aside for major purchases: house, camp, college, renovations, retirement, or illness—nope, you dealt with each major expense as it presented itself. In the early years, he never had the money for these extras. My father had asked his in-laws for a loan for the down payment and was rejected even though they had the money. My father's lifestyle didn't resonate with my grandparents; they had lived through the Depression, worked their whole lives, and saved every penny. My father never forgave them for not having lent him money. He managed to scrape together a down payment and took out a thirty-year mortgage.

I was thrilled with their choice of homes! I carried the floor plans around with me and showed everyone which room would be mine and how it was going to be decorated. In my mind, we would not only be changing homes, but we would also be changing ourselves into the type of family that was illustrated in the brochure. I really believed that we would all watch TV together in the den with the fireplace aglow, have family dinners in the state-of-the-art kitchen, and enjoy holiday meals in the well-appointed dining room. The backyard would be BBQ headquarters on the weekends, and my father would don an apron with a big, puffy white hat to man the grill. Other special effects might include a scampering dog, birds twittering in the trees, and my sister and me sitting on the lawn playing with toys or helping Mom carry delicious side dishes from the kitchen to the wrought-iron patio table. Smiles all around. Suburbia at its most advertised. *Aah, what a wonderful imagination.*

Not surprisingly, our new lifestyle was a major adjustment for each of us, in our own way. My father had it the easiest because he arrived with a network of friends already in place.

His close childhood friend Julie Isaacson, who had grown up with him in Brownsville, had a split-level home just a few blocks away from us. He helped get us established in the new neighborhood by recommending a Chinese restaurant that served good Cantonese food, an appetizing store that sold excellent lox and sturgeon, a bagel store that baked the best bagels and onion bialys, and a deli that had pastrami that was just okay but served impressive stuffed *kishka* ("stuffed derma" in Yiddish . . . best if I don't even explain!).

Julie was the president of the International Doll, Toy, and Novelty Workers Union. He was one of those larger-than-life characters who liked to mingle with celebrities, particularly sports figures. In the late 1950s, when boxing was king, Julie was the manager of heavyweight boxing great Ernie Terrell. Terrell went fifteen rounds in a match against Muhammad Ali at the Astrodome on February 6, 1967. Ali won by a unanimous decision after he viciously pounded Terrell for calling him by his pre-Muslim name, Cassius Clay.

In 1960 it was Julie who became Roger Maris's bestie when the baseball star arrived from Kansas City. I remember the apartment that Julie had found for him in Queens, alongside the Van Wyck Expressway, close to Shea Stadium. I also remember Julie bringing Maris to our house in 1965, where he gave me a signed baseball as my father gave me a brief biography of this living baseball legend.

***

My dad and Julie had shared many adventures since their old days in Brownsville. Perhaps the most notable was in March 1966 when they appeared as witnesses before a federal grand jury in Chicago that was investigating mob influence in boxing.

Organized crime had a history of involvement in the boxing world, but it was not until after the February 1964 boxing match in Miami Beach between relative newcomer twenty-two-year-old Cassius Clay and world heavyweight champion Sonny Liston that a formal federal investigation was launched. With seven-to-one odds against him, Clay knocked out Liston after six rounds, which led many to conclude that such an upset could only have been fixed. It was believed that Ash Resnick, a Las Vegas bookie who was known to have strong ties to organized crime, was influential in throwing the fight.[14]

A rematch between Ali (who had already given up the name Cassius Clay) and Liston was held on May 25, 1965, in Lewiston, Maine, and it seemed to confirm that the fights were being controlled. Halfway through the first round of the match, Liston threw a left jab, Ali countered with a fast right, and Liston went down. The problem was that many did not see Ali's "phantom punch," as it became known. Furthermore, there were issues with how the countdown was conducted. Once again it was believed that the fight had been manipulated, either by the mob or by the Nation of Islam, which was backing Ali.

After Lewiston, Congress launched an investigation into organized crime's influence into the boxing world. My father and Julie were subpoenaed and flew to Chicago to appear before the grand jury. The newspapers described my father as a "reputed New York gambler" and Julie as "Ernie Terrell's former manager." The investigation was ultimately unable to determine any wrongdoing.[15]

While googling my father, I came across a vintage photo of him on Amazon. He was thirty-eight years old and handsome in his dark suit and tie. He has a disgusted look on his face. The back of the photo is marked "John Novick in boxing probe." I bought the photo, which was taken by one of the newspapers covering the trial. I look so much like him.

Julie Isaacson died of cancer in July 2008. His slow deterioration from the disease was very hard for my father, who feared that sickness and death loomed in his near future as well. He could not bring himself to go to Julie's funeral.

---

14. Thom Loverro, "FBI Suspected Iconic 1964 Ali-Liston Fight Was Rigged by Mob," *Washington Times*, February 24, 2014.
15. "Boxing Probe Avoids Press," *Ottawa Herald*, March 31, 1966.

My father blamed his absence in our lives on his commuting time to the other boroughs and, more importantly, his need to work even harder than before to afford our new home. I wanted to believe it all. When I asked him to spend time with me, he would take me along on stops. I would sit in the car while he would visit whomever for whatever amount of time it took.

On one occasion I sat alone in the car on a street off the Bowery with the window cracked open for air while my father went upstairs to a club where he played cards for money. I was so frightened that I was crying when he returned, but there was no soothing words or apology. He had business to do, and I needed to stop acting like a baby.

On Sundays, his self-appointed day off, following a long breakfast accompanied by the *Daily News* and *New York Times*, he made his calls. He spent hours on the yellow wall telephone in the kitchen, making notes on his legal pad, incommunicado with the rest of the family. In the afternoon, when the sport of the season began, he was glued to one or two televisions set up in the den. My mother and I were always welcome to join him provided we kept quiet. No guests in their favorite teams' shirts were ever invited for an afternoon of chili and beer.

Football, baseball, and basketball were not spectator sports at the Novick home; they were a business.

When my father had winners, he smiled, joked, and paid attention to us at dinner. Often, he expressed his delight in song. His repertoire consisted of Yale University's football song "Boola Boola" and Doris Day's 1960s hit "Sleepy Lagoon."

In his winner's stupor, my father would flash my mother a mock romantic look, and rather than sing the correct lyrics, he would unintentionally croon his version of the lyrics, "A slimy lagoon, a tropical moon."

My father added another level of disdain to my becoming a sports fan with these words of advice: "Lisa, you really need to sit and watch the games with me. No guy is going to want to marry you if you don't understand football."

"Thanks, Dad. I'll pass on the football and take my chances that someone might take pity on me and want to spend the rest of their life with a sports imbecile."

Another item to add to my already bulging suitcase of topics for eventual psychotherapy.

My father would often promise to come home early to share a family dinner, but just as often, he arrived after my sister and I had gone to bed. There was always an excuse the next day, no matter how ridiculously insulting it was to us all. My mother and I would make fun of his preposterous stories. We would often concoct our own explanation for his lateness to save him the trouble.

"You're not going to believe what happened tonight," my father might say. "These things could only happen to me! I left the city at six p.m. to come home for dinner, but the Barnum & Bailey Circus is in town. Did you know that? You knew that, Lisa, didn't you? And son of a gun, some elephants got loose on the Grand Central Parkway, and traffic just stood still. Bumper-to-bumper traffic, until they herded them all back into trucks! Was there anything on the news about it? Just my luck."

My dad did make a few attempts to fulfill my vision of suburban family life, but let's just say, he wasn't cut out for the part. One Sunday, both my parents decided to take a stab at real suburban living by deciding to plan a BBQ. I had begged my father to buy a grill so that we could have the family BBQ of my fantasy. We went to the Times Square Store near the JFK airport and bought a small, flimsy grill; a huge bag of charcoal briquettes; and enough lighter fluid to ignite the entire South Shore of Long Island. My dream had included a big brick grill like the one our neighbor had built by hand for his family in their backyard, but I was in no position to be picky.

My dad, dressed in his black pants and sleeveless ribbed undershirt, didn't have a clue as to how to get the coals red and hot in preparation for cooking. As it started to turn dark outside and we all complained about being hungry, any enjoyment or enthusiasm that he might have had with his new role . . . was gone. My mother and sister retreated to the house and ate grilled cheese sandwiches (made on the stovetop), but I supported my dad by standing next to him, a small plastic flashlight in hand pointed at the grill.

I cheered him on as he finally picked up one hot dog with his hands and placed it on the grill as a test. After five minutes of the two of us staring at the hot dog, willing it to cook, my father deemed it ready. He skewered it with a long wood-handled fork and held it up to the light beam for inspection. We both watched in horror as the hot dog fell off the fork and onto the cement patio. I could not believe my seven-year-old eyes as he washed off the hot dog in my sister's plastic wading pool, which was filled with a few inches of water and an assortment of dead bugs. He then contemplated returning it back to the grill. I shook my head with sympathetic disgust and said, "No, Daddy, don't do it. Throw out the hot dog, Daddy. It's okay, you tried."

I felt sorry for him. He gave the pathetic-looking frankfurter to a stray cat that had been hovering around our yard, somehow knowing how it would all end. He and I went into the house to grab something for dinner, and the grill was put in the garage, never to be used again.

***

Upon our arrival in North Woodmere, my mother's to-do list consisted of enrolling me in school, finding a *haimshe* supermarket (Yiddish for "homey, familiar," or Jewish style, e.g., Waldbaum's supermarket was haimshe; the A&P supermarket most definitely was not), scouting out a hairdresser who could tease her black hair sky high, and hiring help for the house.

The supermarket and beauty parlor requirements were settled fairly easily. The help, not so much.

My father urged my mother to hire a live-in maid to help care for my toddler sister and me and to also serve as a companion. A steady stream of southern black women interviewed at our home, and I assisted in the selection process. I liked them all. I thought that anyone who was hired would help relieve my mother's stress, which might ultimately stop the fighting between my parents.

A few women were temporarily employed by us until my mother decided that live-in help was not the way to go. She eventually hired Cherry, a large, very black-skinned woman who had the biggest feet I had ever seen. Cherry was originally from Georgia, or as she called it, "down south." She commuted to us from Brooklyn on the Long Island Railroad three times a week. We never knew how old she was, and there was no way of telling; she could have been forty or seventy. Her skin was as smooth as silk from applying Vaseline to her face every night, her beauty secret. Cherry never raised her voice and seemed to be perpetually at peace with herself. I knew that she had another life, but I am embarrassed to say that for a child as aware as I was, I didn't have a clue as to what that life apart consisted of. Did she have a husband? Children? Did she grow up with a mother and father? Did she live in a house or an apartment? Was she tired when she got home after a long day's work? What did she do on the weekends? Did she love us? Did she like us? I only knew that Cherry made the best fried chicken and BBQ ribs in the world and that she always had a smile and kind words for me and that I loved her and appreciated her for how she made me feel. She represented quiet and predictability. My Cherry seemed much happier than I was.

My mother enrolled me in Ogden Elementary School, located in the very desirable District 14 school system. I had my own challenges adapting to our new life out of Brooklyn. I arrived at Ogden in mid-May 1965, just weeks before the end of the term. My mother parked our car in a circular driveway in front of a new, one-story, light-colored brick building. The trees were in bloom, and flowers were planted along the perimeter of the entrance. I was escorted into another world when I entered Mrs. Rosenblum's first-grade class, dressed in my crisp yellow-and-white summer party dress with white patent leather shoes. I remember thinking that the kids and even the teacher were all dressed so casually; some were even in sneakers! The whole class eyed me, and I was terrified. Not only was I dressed so differently than the others, but I also stood heads above my classmates. My height proved traumatic throughout elementary school, even costing me my sixth-grade school dance date, who opted for a more compact-sized girl. I was always positioned at the back of the line and the back of the classroom. I was always given the adult parts in school plays, and I was oddly expected to be more mature and behave "bigger" as a result of my size. And so, I did. It wasn't until middle school that my gawkiness transformed into litheness and my schoolmates had their growth spurts that this issue became a nonissue.

On that first day at Ogden, the class was rehearsing for *The Frog Prince*, the play that it was going to perform in front of the school later that month. The princess, Caryn Gartenberg, wore a gold plastic tiara in her hair and carried a medium-sized bouncing ball that had been painted gold. The frog prince, Robert Gutner, hopped around a plastic kiddie pool that had been painted green to resemble a pond. The kids were all talking and laughing, and there I was, standing in disbelief as if I had fallen through the looking glass. Due to my late arrival on the scene, Mrs. Rosenblum cast me as a village peasant. That was the least of my problems.

Thanks to my father and his friend Alley the furrier, come winter, my sister and I were the envy of the elementary-school fashion set. With the first nippy breeze, we donned our beautiful white rabbit-skin jackets. These were no ratty-looking pelts but rather luxuriously soft, hooded, and zippered garments trimmed in fabric.

As an adolescent, I received and proudly wore a brown mink hat that made me look like I was wearing a dead marmoset on my head. But it was fur and it was free. Enough said.

I have since made my peace with my PETA transgressions.

I discovered that suburban kids were expected to entertain themselves just like we had in Brooklyn. My mother encouraged my creative process with such delightful expressions as "You're bored? Go play in traffic." Or "You're bored? Go bang your head against the wall." Or "You're bored? Take a long walk off a short pier."

I made friends with the kids who had moved into our new development. The Valley Stream dump, though no longer active, served as a great playground. We climbed on hills of dirt scattered with junk that included old bottles, rebar, shoes, and an occasional appliance. We chased one another while pretending to be characters from *The Man from U.N.C.L.E.* and *Get Smart*, using portable radios with antennas that doubled as spy-worthy walkie-talkies. We saw the rats scamper at dusk in our garbage kingdom and taunted one another with the possibility of an encounter. At dusk, our mothers' screams signaled that it was time to return home for our baths and other bedtime rituals.

After school, I took ballet lessons in Miss Dolores's small and smelly basement (no exits other than a few small ceiling windows) along with my friend. My awkward adolescent body refused to bend gracefully into a plié or any of the other contortions. I can still hear Miss Dolores (today she would be known as Ms. Dolores) shouting at me, "*Allonge*, Lisa, *allonge!*" (or "Lengthen, Lisa, lengthen"). Even at that age, I saw the ridiculousness in the whole setup; Miss Dolores was from Brooklyn! Her fancy French words didn't fool me! My feet did not fare well in tap shoes, either; my step-ball-change and shuffle, shuffle, shuffle were lackluster. It was clear that I would have to shine in another field.

When I was in sixth grade, we were gifted an upright piano from someone in the record industry, and I asked for piano lessons. My friend Cindy's mom, who appeared to me to be very smart and capable, was always talking about having gone to Vassar College. Since I didn't have anyone close to me who went to college, I drank in all her stories. I wanted to be a Vassar girl too someday. I asked my parents if I could take piano lessons because I had seen photos of smiling Vassar coeds lounging around a piano in their dorm living room, and I mentally placed myself in the cozy scene. I needed to learn to play piano. I needed Vassar girl credentials.

Mr. Spero was a short, square-shaped man who resembled SpongeBob SquarePants in a suit. He showed up every Friday afternoon with his briefcase filled with sheet music. He took an immediate liking to my mother, which at first made me nauseous and, later, plain old angry. At the end of the hour lesson, we would switch places on the piano bench, and he would show off to my mom by playing a medley of show tunes. His stubby fingers flew across the piano keys as he hammered out the notes to "Moon River" and the *Finian's Rainbow* theme. He tried to woo her with "Raindrops Keep Fallin' on My Head," a blockbuster song at the time. I would always wish that he would just pack up his briefcase and go home to Mrs. Spero, but no such luck. Did he expect us to join him in a rousing chorus from *Oklahoma!* or *Brigadoon*?

I wished that my dad would come home unexpectedly during one of my lessons and teach Mr. Spero a lesson! I waited until I was proficient at playing Burt Bacharach's "Promises, Promises," and then I quit piano lessons. I'd have to find another way to become a Vassar girl!

It was the first of many instruments, sports, languages, and jobs for which I showed promise but chose not to stick it out.

A few years later my father came home with a beautiful Martin steel-string guitar given to him by Lionel Hampton. The connection between these men could only have been the record industry (I'll fill you in later).

Our neighborhood was 99.9 percent Jewish, and if I wanted to fit in with the other kids, I needed to get my Jewish on! I was envious of the kids who went to synagogue with their parents. To me, it meant that those families were part of the community, and it also meant that the parents cared enough about their children to insist that they get a Jewish education. I remember that my mother sent me to elementary school on Rosh Hashanah and Yom Kippur. It was only me and Peter Antholzer in the class; everyone else stayed home and observed the holidays with their families! I cried and begged, and still my mother insisted. What was going on there? I wanted to go to synagogue just like the other kids.

With no help from anyone, I started to learn about what it meant to be Jewish. I remained fascinated with the memory of growing up so close to the Lubavitcher community in Crown Heights. I longed to celebrate the Jewish New Year known as Rosh Hashanah, the Festival of Lights called Hanukkah, and Passover, which commemorates the Jewish slaves' exodus from Egypt.

I was jealous of the kids who said that they couldn't come out to play just as the sun was setting on the eve of the holidays because they were waiting for relatives to arrive with armloads of gifts and special foods. I wanted to be just like my classmates whose mothers had set their beautiful dining room tables with lace tablecloths and napkins, delicate china plates and bowls, crystal glasses, and sterling silver utensils, all of which had been passed down from some great-grandma or aunt. I wanted to light tall, tapered candles placed in carefully polished silver holders that had made a long, hard trip to the table from the old country. I wanted their light to cast a beautiful glow that everyone could see from the street.

One year I came home crying because I wanted to have a seder for Passover like everyone else in the neighborhood. My father was not at home, but my grandparents, who were visiting, were clearly touched by my sadness. My grandmother set the kitchen table with our mismatched plates and glasses from S&H Green Stamps, put a candle in a tin holder, and located the Maxwell House Haggadah that was given for free at the supermarket with our grocery purchases. My grandpa led the seder and read the stories that had been told for generations.

I was probably the only child who wanted to go to Hebrew school; I commiserated with my friends when they complained about having to go twice a week after public school, but secretly I wished that I was joining them. One Sunday when I was eight years old, I walked the short distance by myself to Rabbi and Rebbetzin Jungreis's house, which was temporarily being used as the synagogue, or shul. I marched myself into the Sunday school classroom and took a seat. The young teachers had no idea why I was there since I was not registered, but they gave me a textbook and allowed me stay . . . and I did, for several weeks, until the teacher finally came to me and said that I must have my parents pay the fee if I wanted to continue. I was so embarrassed. Why didn't my parents know about these things? Everyone else's parents knew! Why didn't they care enough about me to insist that I go to Hebrew school? Why didn't they want to be Jewish?

My participation in the class meant that my family would have to join the synagogue, Ohr Torah, which was then under construction. My parents didn't want to join the congregation (perhaps because of the cost), and I never set foot in another temple until it was time to attend my friends' Bar Mitzvahs when we were thirteen years old.

Our Jewish connection did not go beyond our Sunday morning bagel-and-lox ritual, with one exception: my dad always fasted on Yom Kippur. Yom Kippur, the holiest day of the Jewish year observed by even the most secular Jewish men and women, is known as the Day of Atonement. It is the day that God determines your fate, and it is marked by intense prayer in synagogue, introspection, atonement for your year's past deeds, and a twenty-five-hour fast from food and drink.

Every year, my father submitted to God's commandment. To take his mind off the kitchen and to help make the day pass quickly, he would stay in bed watching television and talking on the phone (both infractions). The fast ends at nightfall, the exact time noted in the Jewish calendar and celebrated with the blowing of the shofar (ram's horn) in synagogue. Rather than use these indicators, my father chose (assuming it had been a sunny day) to station himself outside on the lawn in the front of our house, barefoot and in his torn bathrobe, with his hair sticking straight up on top of his head, to check the position of the sun in the sky.

He would stand there with one hand shielding his eyes from the glare of the setting sun, striking a pose like a portly Hiawatha. With the other hand, he held closed his bathrobe as he watched until the ball of light sunk below the tops of the trees and houses to the west. The streets of North Woodmere substituted for the shores of Gitche Gumee. Our neighbors, looking tired and hungry as they walked home from shul, tried not to stare or be judgmental (after all, it was Yom Kippur), though they sneaked quick glances in disbelief. I would watch the scene in horror from the front door, begging him to come inside with the enticement of a table full of whitefish, baked salmon salad, smoked salmon (nova and belly lox), vegetable cream cheese, bagels, and bialys.

Despite my dad's glaring transgressions, I was proud of his observance. For once, we Novicks were somewhat like everyone else, rather than like the strange Munster family of TV fame. I was able to join my friends in conversation about how they spent the holiday. More importantly, my father's actions showed me that despite his seemingly omnipotent, rules-don't-apply-to-him behavior, he understood that there was a power greater than himself. He and I never discussed why he chose to recognize the sanctity of the day; I am sure he had a bunch of reasons that even he wasn't fully aware of. There was one incident, however, that occurred when I was about twelve years old and gave me insight into his motives.

I walked into the bedroom on Yom Kippur while Dad was on the phone with one of his friends, reviewing the football game lineup for the coming weekend. As part of my father's conversation sign-off, he said laughingly, "I'm going to spend the day praying for [sports] winners."

I looked at him, and I was embarrassed to have heard his words. He looked at me, and he was clearly embarrassed for what he had said, or maybe he was clearly embarrassed for what he got caught saying. I quickly walked out of the room. Was there nothing that frightened my dad? Wasn't he afraid that God would punish him for not having respect for the holiness of the day? I will never forget that time, when so much was said between us without saying a word.

When my mother was feeling well, she was able to play her role as the suburban mom. She was a good cook, and we girls would eat delicious dinners together at the kitchen table while watching *The Munsters* and *McHale's Navy*. She would take us to Brooklyn to visit our grandparents, to lunch at Howard

Johnson's, to shop at the Green Acres Mall, and to and from our friends' houses when we couldn't ride our bikes. Despite the numerous problems between me and my mother, I knew that she provided the only regularity that my sister and I knew. We went to school, did our homework, and had dinner followed by a strict bedtime. She was the one who gave our lives structure.

As part of my mother's attempts to fit into the suburban mom mold, she frequently volunteered to be the class mother on several of my sister's and my school field trips, including to the post office, the Jamaica Bay Wildlife Refuge, and Farmingdale Farm. She left her unique mark on each outing.

One of the most memorable trips was when she joined us on my ninth-grade earth science class trip to hunt for fossils at the Palisades cliffs overlooking the Hudson River. It was an overcast day in May, and all the kids had on their dungarees and work boots and were armed with hammers to pry loose our own little pieces of the Triassic Period. My mother met us in the school parking lot dressed as if she were off to a day in the city rather than a trip hunting for prehistoric souvenirs. She wore beige slacks, a white button-down silk blouse, and white patent leather platform shoes, carrying a white leather pocketbook. She was perhaps at the height of her beauty in those days, with shoulder-length black hair, dark skin, and a curvy shape. I thought that my teachers, both geeky men in sensible shoes with slide rules sticking out of their short-sleeved button-down shirts, were going to need resuscitation! The boys on the bus began to fight over who would be in her group for the day. I have photos of the teachers holding her arms and helping her navigate the muddy paths as they vied for her attention instead of guiding the expedition. Even the bus driver got in on the action! When we took a lunch break at the Red Apple Rest along the New York State Thruway, the teachers carried her tray to the table, then ate and laughed with her until it was time to go. The other class mothers were not amused. I was so proud of her. For once I was glad that she wasn't anything like the other mothers.

Another trip was to the Museum of Modern Art in Manhattan. It was a sunny day in the late fall, and we were all looking forward to escaping the classroom and going into the city to see the paintings that we had been studying. During the bus ride, the teacher broke us up into four groups with each mother as a leader. We were given instructions on where to find each of the paintings that we would later have to write about, but other than that, our time at the museum was our own. My mother, once again looking "hot," announced to our group that our tour would start in the museum café—she needed coffee to be an effective leader. The group spent the next forty-five minutes talking at a table with sodas and pastries, her treat. My mother never left the café, and our group went off on our own to see the Andy Warhol exhibit.

CHAPTER 13

I HAD A TOUGH TIME

Despite her efforts, my mother's anxious and depressive nature worsened in those early years; she just could not sustain feeling good for any length of time. With my father rarely at home, she was not mentally equipped to handle the stress of single parenthood. She went through the motions of caring for my sister and me, but she was emotionally detached. She served us dinner at five o'clock, then prepared my sister for bed while I did homework and watched television in the den by myself. My mother would go into her room, sometimes to watch TV, but many times to just lie in the darkness. I felt sad for her and for me, too, but mostly I felt anger. I wanted desperately to be like the other kids whose families ate meals together and watched television and rode bicycles and took vacations to Colonial Williamsburg or Expo 67 or went on Christmas vacation to visit their nanas and papas in Miami Beach. Why didn't she go to a psychiatrist like my father was always telling her to do? Why wasn't she like the other moms who spent their days with their girlfriends having lunch or shopping or playing mah-jongg or planning dinner parties? Why was she so mean? Why couldn't I make her happy?

On many occasions when I was still in elementary school, I would be awoken by my parents screaming when my father finally did come home. My mother would have prepared a meal for him at the time that he said he would be home. Hours later, when he had still not arrived, his food was ice cold and she was steaming hot. She did try. She would already be in bed, and he couldn't understand why she wouldn't come down to serve him. Sometimes, he came home late at night with cases of food such as sirloin steaks, South African lobster tails, and restaurant-sized cheesecakes, luxury foods that had probably "fallen off the back of a truck." We had a freezer in the garage that bulged with gourmet goodies. The cases had to be opened, the food wrapped and prepared for the freezer. My mother would protest by refusing to get out of bed, and my father would scream, which would wake me up. Ultimately, I did the work, which left me with a jumble of exhausting emotions. I was angry that they did not care enough and had woken me. I was angry that I was being used by them to get at each other. I was sad that they resorted to such un-grown-up-like behavior and were neither embarrassed nor sorry. I also felt guilt. Had I done something to make them like this? Was I doing something wrong as a child to make them feel that it was okay to treat me this way?

My parents' late-night fights left me tired and anxious for the next school morning. By the third grade, I was regularly visiting the school nurse to deal with stomach pains or take a quick nap. I found it hard to concentrate in class and complete my homework in the evenings. My class grades were underwhelming compared with the results of my aptitude scores. I also began to make up very descriptive stories of how I wished my life would be rather than how it was. When we studied about Maine, I told my classmates that I had gone there over the summer with my family. Not true. I would often tell my teacher, Mrs. Hochman, about my parents' arguments. She would listen sympathetically, but there was a whole different mind-set in the mid-1960s; the schools did not get involved in a student's personal life. Mrs. Hochman's kindness, patience, and recognition of my capabilities helped carry me through a particularly painful year.

When I was about nine years old, my parents left my sister and me alone for the first time with Cherry while they went on a junket to Las Vegas. The day before, they had a big argument that left me so upset that I lay in my bed with an ice pack on my head to take away the headache that had developed from sobbing for so many hours. But somehow, they were able to get past their anger for each other and reconcile just in time to leave for Vegas. To them, it was as if nothing had happened— it was just another blowout with no consequences. Neither of them had apologized to me for what they had put me through. I don't think that it ever occurred to them. I sat on the floor of my room when they came in to say goodbye. They were both dressed smartly, Dad in a suit and Mom in a dress, looking as glamorous as the celebrities and showgirls that she would soon be seeing. No one was threatening to slit anyone's throat as they had been just a day earlier.

They both were clearly excited about leaving. *Leaving me?* I wondered.

I got angrier and angrier knowing that they really could control themselves if they wanted to. They tried to give me a kiss goodbye, but I refused to even look up at them as I pretended to read a book. I wanted to hit them and curse at them and tell them that I hoped that they would die in an airplane crash. I wanted to punish them any way that I could for hurting me. And I did all those things . . . in my mind. I would show them what it was like to be able to control oneself. I would show them that even though they were my parents, I was the one who acted more maturely. I waited until I heard them get into the taxi before peeking out my window and watching them drive down the block. I didn't know what to do with all my rage, so I cried.

After they left, overwhelming guilt settled in. Would I ever see them again? What if I had wished my parents dead and they died? I made deals with God that if he kept my mother and father safe, I would never be angry at them again, nor would I ever give them any reason to be angry with me. No matter what.

***

The fear over losing my parents to an untimely death became obsessive by the time I was entering junior high school. My fear was particularly centered on my father. Without a clear picture of an office where he worked or what he did all day, my mind filled the void with visions of him out in the streets of New York, a target for all the evils that my overstimulated imagination could conjure up. There was nothing about my father that even hinted at vulnerability, but to me, he was out there in the thick of it all with no one to protect him. Had Prozac been invented, it would have really helped me, but in its absence, my anxiety robbed me of a lot of carefree childhood time.

The world was a very scary place for me; I envisioned all types of things that could hurt my parents. This obsession with their safety went on for years as my anger at them recycled itself as fear of losing them. Since I led an uncensored childhood, I watched the nightly news and combed through the latest issues of *Life* and *Look* magazines with their graphic photos of the violence that seemed to me to be eating up the world in the 1960s. I was horrified by the photos that depicted the Vietnam War, including prisoners of war being tortured, the now iconic shot of a South Vietnamese police chief executing a Vietcong collaborator with a gun held to the side of his head, and the aftermath of the Tet Offensive. I cried over Gordon Parks's black-and-white photos of the plight of the poor Negro in America and at the images of the bloated, starving bodies of the children caught up in the civil war in Biafra. I was terrified that either the Black Panthers or Charles Manson would come and kill us white pigs.

On our visits to the city, I looked out the car window at runaway kids, not much older than myself, many who had left comfortable homes and families just like mine, to become addicted to drugs and live their dangerous, dirty lives on the streets of St. Mark's Place in the East Village. At school we watched a choppy reel-to-reel film of an American Indian crying at how we were ruining our planet with pollution and garbage. In bed at night, I listened as a car with a speaker mounted on its roof drove around the streets of our otherwise silent neighborhood, appealing to the community to donate money to help the Israelis fight the Arabs in what became known as the Six-Day War.

My parents' crazy and immature behavior made my world feel even more uncertain and terrifying. I wanted my parents to protect me from things that I couldn't understand and that frightened me, but it was my parents who frightened me the most. Since I was the one who acted like the parent, who was going to protect me?

The panic would begin after school; I couldn't relax or concentrate on my homework or participate in after-school activities until my father phoned home and I spoke to him. The problem was that he never called at a regular time or sometimes not at all, despite my pleas to get him to do so. Reliability would have been reassuring, but his response was "Lisa, stop being silly. I can't always get to a phone. I call when I can. Sometimes I am in traffic or a meeting or a card game. I don't have the same schedule as the other fathers do. Do you understand that I have to support all of us? It's a lot of stress, Lisa."

Of course, he was right. I was being unreasonable. I absolutely did not want to give him more pressure. Didn't my mother give him enough of that? He was always telling me that she was going to give him a heart attack. I didn't want to make the demand that would kill him! Instead, I asked him if I could look forward to one night each week that I knew he'd come home for dinner followed by watching TV together. I didn't care if we watched what he chose; I just wanted to be with him. He said that he would try. And he did, if only for a couple of weeks.

I knew deep inside that my father was not home much because he chose not to be. It was obvious he didn't enjoy family time. It was far too boring in its predictability, and besides, all he did was fight with my mother. But no matter what he did or didn't do, I found it nearly impossible to stay angry with him. I needed to believe in at least one of my parents, and because he played the proverbial good cop, I chose him. Ostensibly, he was the more grown up of the two. He had friends and interests and responsibilities. He appeared to handle life's challenges from a position of strength, unlike my mother, whose coping mechanisms included screaming or hiding in bed. I chose to swallow all the anger toward my father and his obvious truth contortions because the alternative was to allow bad feelings to corrupt our time together and fuel an already explosive family situation.

This fear of losing my father was an ongoing, debilitating theme throughout my life.

I began to have nightmares and to walk in my sleep. All my fears were turned inward, so there was no escaping the pain. I had one reoccurring dream that would wake me up terrified and soaked in sweat. The dream was more of a feeling than a visual story. It seemed to go on for a long time, and it wouldn't let me wake up until it was good and ready. I was curled up, being crushed and squeezed until I couldn't breathe.

My hands and feet were clenched so hard that they hurt. I tried to scream, but nobody could hear me. I was finally released into whiteness, gasping and crying. Sometimes the dream was so frightening that I would call for my father to come into my room. Mostly he and my mother would tell me from their bed to just roll over and go back to sleep, that it was nothing. There were times that I couldn't shake off the feeling, and I would just lie in my bed until morning, my heart pounding, fearful of the day ahead.

The dream went on intermittently for years. I was still in elementary school when I asked my parents to take me to see a psychiatrist. In retrospect, I not only wanted to alleviate some of my pain, but I also wanted to be an example to my mother for what she needed to do for herself. My mother refused to take me to see a doctor, claiming that psychiatrists made kids worse . . . once you went into therapy, they never let you out. Or perhaps she was frightened that I would tell an outsider what was going on at home?

My beautiful room was my refuge. My grandparents had bought me white princess furniture trimmed in gold when we moved into the new house. I was the only one of my friends to have a full-size bed, which I covered with a yellow bedspread and my stuffed animals. The glossy wallpaper had large red, white, yellow, and pink flowers outlined in black. I swept my red shag carpeting daily and made sure the room was always clean and orderly. I had a yellow princess phone and a small TV on the dresser, the envy of all my friends. There were white shutters on the windows, and outside were window boxes stuffed with artificial plants and flowers. A family of squirrels once made their home in the boxes, and the loud chattering would wake me in the morning. When I wasn't teaching my imaginary class, I was listening to records, reading Nancy Drew books, and organizing my international postcard collection. I had a psychedelic-colored poster on the back of my door that read "March to the Beat of Your Own Drum."

By fifth grade, I developed a set of strict standards that gave me the structure and predictability that I needed. I started to take my schoolwork seriously. I made sure that I did my assignments, studied for my tests, did extra-credit work when possible, and read all types of books, including those on the bookshelves in our den such as *In Cold Blood* and *Valley of the Dolls*. I played school for hours in the makeshift classroom that I set up in my bedroom, complete with a large blackboard, a pointer, maps, and even a pupil—my sister. I turned my anger and frustration inward with an obsessive drive for perfection. Since I couldn't control the craziness that surrounded me, I was dead set on controlling whatever I could.

I'd spend hours writing a composition, mulling over each word and the placement of each sentence to make sure that my message would be clearly understood. My schoolwork became my identity, and I put my concern for my grades on par with the concern of a chairman of the board of a Fortune 500 company for the release of quarterly earnings. In middle school, I was the captain of the volleyball team. In camp, I held the lead role in every play and won every all-camp award for which I was eligible. I was a star. I was also scared and exhausted.

My desperation found a comfortable outlet in another obsession—my weight. I counted every calorie in my strictly planned meals, every raisin in my bowl of cereal in order to gain some form of control over my life. At times I couldn't get to sleep at night because I was so hungry, but the payoff was that I loved the way I looked, if not the way I felt. I was motivated by my belief that being pretty would be my ticket away from my parents. We were such a food-oriented family that I felt it was a good way to rebel. I wanted to show them that I was different than them in every way; I could control myself even if they could not. Anorexia was not a disease we had heard about in those days, but in retrospect, that was exactly what I had. My food obsession really got to my parents, which I think was the hidden objective. Eating was something near and dear to them, and they felt that anyone who didn't indulge freely must surely have serious problems. When they finally noticed what was happening to me, they were so concerned that they managed to join forces when confronting me. Control felt so good!

"Lisa, why don't you eat?" my father asked. "Look what you look like. Do you think boys like girls who are that skinny?"

My mother chimed in, "Remember those teenage boys in the restaurant last week? One said that you were pretty, but the other said that you were too skinny. You have linguini legs. You look terrible. You've got to stop this. Come downstairs and eat something. Johnny, tell her she has to eat something."

I wanted to shock them, even if it was just for the moment, into understanding how much pain I was in. I told them that I wanted to be thin and beautiful to get as far away from them as possible just as soon as I was able. The irony was that I didn't want to leave them or hurt them or hate them. I just wanted to love them and have them give me the love that I needed. My explanation destroyed their joint parenting tactic, and they instantly reverted to blaming each other and shifting the attention to themselves. Thankfully, the eating disorder ended not too long after the confrontation. It was less than a year before I was once again a full-fledged member of the Novick eating team.

CHAPTER 14

THOSE WACKY 1970s!

In the early 1970s the fashion world was on steroids and everything was big: shirt lapels, platform shoes and wedges, bell-bottom jeans, sunglasses, women's hair piled high from teasing and wiglets, and men's sideburns shaped long and wide. My father must have also gotten bigger in business because money seemed to be more plentiful. My parents hired a decorator, Yvette, to furnish our home in the popular French provincial style. The oversized red-and-mustard-colored velvet chairs and couches were much more comfortable than the outdoor folding chairs and chaise lounges that had served as our den furniture for years. My parents each drove boat-sized Cadillac Coupe de Villes, he to and from work and she to and from the supermarket, the cleaners, and the bank.

By sixth grade I had gotten my period, was thin and shapely, and was quite taken with myself. My linguini legs had filled out, and I had long, thick hair that I tamed by applying generous amounts of Dippity-Do gel and wrapping it around my head. The hair at the crown was wound around a huge pink roller, or in some cases a beer can, and fastened with oversized silver clips. I had big brown eyes with long dark lashes and bushy eyebrows that my mother tried to contain with brutal tweezing sessions. When I put on my dungaree bell-bottom pants and paired them with a safari shirt and suede fringed vest, there was no stopping me.

I managed to do well socially and academically due to a bit of luck and whole lot of hard work. Thanks to a very strong network of friends and their families, I was able to maintain a life outside my home. My ability to find role models and mentors was crucial to my resilience. I was remarkably capable of bouncing back from regularly occurring traumatic episodes.

I did my best to try to control the demons that were torturing me internally. On the surface, it seemed that I was successful. I was an honors student and had friends from different social groups. I had developed my mom's quick, sarcastic sense of humor, which balanced my overly serious nature. My friends and I went ice-skating at Grant Park, shopping in Cedarhurst, and bowling at Green Acres Mall. We went to the movies at least once a week and then had pizza for dinner followed by a sleepover date. In home economics class, we sewed aprons and learned to make carrot curls while making fun of Mrs. Jacobs, our teacher. We celebrated the beginning and end of the school year and summer camp with giant scoops of homemade ice cream at Walt Itgen's Ice Cream Parlour in Valley Stream.

While in seventh and eighth grades, we attended dozens of Bar and Bat Mitzvahs that we primped for like debutantes preparing for their coming-out parties. We polished our nails, hair-sprayed our banana curls, and tried on a succession of outfits until we looked like the teen models in *Seventeen* and *Ingenue* magazines. We listened to the music of Creedence Clearwater Revival, Three Dog Night, and Joni Mitchell while we talked about boys, looked at pictures of boys, and dreamed of boys.

***

My first time on an airplane was in December 1969 when we went on a junket to the Caribbean island of Curaçao. The junkets were led by a Long Island guy named Louis Katz. Despite being only eleven years old, I planned for the trip like a middle-aged traveler going on a round-the-world adventure. I read again and again the slim brochure from the Curaçao Hilton, which was located on the picturesque Piscadera Bay. I envisioned myself in a brightly colored bikini, stretched out on a lounge chair by the star-shaped pool. I planned my outfits like a countess embarking on a first-class, transatlantic voyage on the *Queen Mary*. I learned what little I could about the island from *The World Book Encyclopedia*: its local language, Papiamento; its Dutch history; its pontoon bridge in the quaint capital, Willemstad; and about rijsttafel, a delicious Indonesian dish adapted by the Dutch.

Despite an occasional parental skirmish, I remember our trips to Curaçao as some of the happiest times we spent together as a family. We each established a daily routine that suited each of our needs. Every morning I would wake up early and quietly put on my bathing suit and go downstairs for breakfast by myself. I'd sit happily at a table by myself and watch other guests. I probably would have read the *New York Times* or the *Wall Street Journal* had they been available! Later in the morning I would go up to the room and check if my sister was awake, dress her, and take her down for breakfast and then to the pool, where we would stay until the late afternoon. My parents would emerge from their room around one o'clock p.m., and we would have lunch together. Dad would then play cards with the other men on the junket, and my mother would usually return to the room. At night we would have a long dinner together, and my sister and I would watch the same show presented nightly in the ballroom while my parents went to the casino. I would take my sister up to the room after the show and get us ready for bed, sometimes treating the painful sun poisoning that we had acquired during our sunscreen-free days in the tropics.

In 1971 we made three trips to the Curaçao Hilton. While I was doing research online for this book, I came across heavily redacted FBI documents on Genovese boss Funzi Tieri. To my surprise, I found the following: "I advised on January 25, 1972, that Frank Tieri . . . described by sources as a big shylock gambler, and who owns a bagel of [sic] pretzel factory in Brooklyn, New York, are negotiating to take over the casino in the Hilton Hotel, Curaçao, West Indies."[16]

While I will never know or care who the adviser was, the redacted name in the report was without a doubt Herbert or John Novick. This might explain why we always got pulled aside at customs and all our bags were overturned and inspected upon our return to JFK International Airport from Curaçao.

***

My anxiety level eased up some when I entered George W. Hewlett High School, class of 1976, and became more preoccupied with myself and my social life and spent more time away from the house and my parents.

Just before I turned sixteen, I met tall and very skinny Teddy Heidrich, who was seventeen and captain of the high school swim and cross-country track teams. In a community that was 99 percent Jewish, I managed to find one of the few boys who wasn't. Teddy was a German Irish, middle-class Methodist. He came from a close, hardworking, flag-waving family who took equal pride in what they did and how they did it. Their small red-painted colonial home was wonderfully chaotic with two dogs, a cat that lived on top of the refrigerator, and kids and friends who were always coming and going.

---

16. Federal Bureau of Investigation, field office file NY 92-2476.

Teddy's father, Mr. H., worked in and later owned an upscale dry cleaning store in Cedarhurst, New York, named Arthur Copeland Cleaners. He was an ex-marine who had fought in the Korean War, and it was immediately clear that the military's discipline and values were ingrained in the family. Mrs. Heidrich had a variety of low-paying jobs, but mostly she ran the house and took care of the four kids. Mr. H. would come home for lunch every day, and he and his wife would spend the hour talking about their morning over a sandwich of cold cuts on white bread, sometimes accompanied by a beer, sometimes a glass of milk. The family would all gather for dinner in the dining room, the dogs obediently sitting under the table.

When the Heidrichs came together, it was the conversation rather than the food that was the center of everyone's attention. *Imagine that?* Before bed, Mr. and Mrs. Heidrich each slowly drank a glass of port wine, said good night to the family, and together climbed the narrow steps to their bedroom.

The differences in our homes was nothing short of tremendous. The Heidrichs were like aliens dropped down from a Hollywood daytime television set when compared with my parents. Plus, the differences between the Jewish home and Gentile home were no less than monumental. Mrs. Heidrich kept their butter in a dish on the counter in the kitchen where it oozed into a shiny yellow lump. A Jewish mother would never ever keep the butter out of the refrigerator, fearing that she would be sentencing her family to a slow, excruciating gastrointestinal death! And yet, the Heidrichs remained strong and healthy. *Amazing.*

I was madly in love with Teddy and everything he and his family stood for. They included me as one of their own, and I spent every minute possible in their company, making a mental inventory of how I would act when Ted and I were married with a family of our own.

My parents were very happy with my choice of boyfriend. He was included in almost of all our family activities, which were always outside the home and usually involved eating. My father saw it as a challenge to get Ted to try different foods and fatten up. Much to his delight, Teddy took easily to our love of Chinese and Italian food, and even traditional Jewish dishes. He did draw the line at tasting gefilte fish, a gelatinous white-fish and pike composite with roots in Eastern Europe. Served with horseradish and a carrot, a lump of gefilte fish on the plate of one uninitiated to the delicacy was known to make even the toughest man gag in refusal to taste.

Believing that Ted would someday be his son-in-law, my father introduced him to a world of money and all that it could facilitate. Ted and I are still close, and he recently shared a story of which I was unaware. Ted was in his junior year at the State University of New York at Plattsburgh when he and my father had the following conversation.

"Teddy, whattaya going to do with yourself after gradua-tion?" my dad asked.

"I'm an accounting major. I'm thinking about becoming a CPA," Ted responded.

"Accounting? Forget it. No money in accounting. Here's what you're going to do," said my dad with his usual bang-you-over-the-head subtlety. "I've got two options for you. First, and I think this should be your choice, I can arrange to get you a liquor distributorship. Your territory is protected. You can make a lot of money, and you work, let's say, maybe from eight a.m. until eleven a.m. Or you can be an inspector on the docks. Starting pay is around thirty-five thousand dollars." Just for perspective, the average college professor was making around $14,000 in those years!

Teddy said, "John, I really appreciate it, but I'm still in school, and I've got loans."

My father didn't hesitate. "Quit. Quit and declare bankruptcy. It's not a problem, believe me."

Teddy politely declined the offers; married a girl from Missouri; moved to Lewiston, Maine; remained an officer in the marine reserves; had two beautiful children; and became a very successful insurance agent.

Had he gone along with my father's plan . . . I calculated that right about now he would be getting out of prison!

Ted and I remained a couple for the first few years in college, and then in the late 1970s, he marched off to marine officers' training camp at Camp Lejeune, and I marched off to summers in Europe. We remain good friends to this day.

***

My sweet sixteen was held in May 1974 at the Valley Stream Park Inn. I was dressed in a floral high-necked dress that made me look like a cross between an Amish woman and the 1970s TV character Mary Hartman played by Louise Lasser. The party, though modest in comparison to others that I attended, was not to my father's liking. He was unhappy with the final cost for the sweet sixteen and that the event interfered with a baseball game that he wanted to watch. He was uninhibited in displaying his displeasure, frequently leaving the party room the entire afternoon to get his scores. He planted himself near the dance floor, studying everyone suspiciously through his dark sunglasses, arms crossed over his chest with a scowl on his face. As if I wasn't uncomfortable enough with his behavior, Mark Brooks came up to me and said with sarcasm, "Lisa, your dad looks like such a jolly guy! A real load of laughs! Does he have to wear those sunglasses in here? He looks like a hit man!"

I begged my mother to say something to my father.

"John, you're scaring all the kids," she said. "Take off those sunglasses. You look ridiculous."

He responded, "Don't tell me what to do!"

They were off and running.

***

In my senior year of high school, my guidance counselor, Mrs. Nadler, called me into her office to tell me about an article that *Newsday*, Long Island's newspaper, was writing entitled "Teenage Girls Today: The 'Can Do' Generation." She had been approached by a young writer, Tony Kornheiser (who later became a famous sports talk radio host), to see if she had any candidates to recommend. During a free period, along with Teddy, I met Tony at the nearby Burger King for the interview. I was completely honest about how I felt as a young woman about to be graduating and leaving home for college.

The article came out on March 14, 1976, in Sunday's newspaper magazine section. The piece on me began:

> Lisa Novick is one of those girls who appear to hold the world like a yo-yo, spinning at their pleasure. She lives with her parents and younger sister in comfortable, middle-class North Woodmere, and her parents give her all the freedom she can handle. Her schoolwork seems to come easily, and she got a 94 average at Hewlett High School, where she's on the yearbook staff, the archery team and the prom committee. She's got a steady boyfriend and her own car. Her senior profile is suitable for framing. She's never even smoked pot.

But don't tell her how good she's got it.
Don't tell her that being 17 is worth all the
fried chicken in Kentucky. Because she
doesn't think it's such a bargain.

The first time that I saw the article was that Sunday when my father picked up five copies of the *Newsday* along with the *New York Times* and our bagel breakfast. My parents each took a copy, and with one look at their faces, I knew how disappointed they were in me.

"It's not a nice article, Lisa," my dad said. "Not nice at all. Makes you look like you don't know what you're doing."

"He's right," my mother said while chomping on her bagel.

They put away the article and went quietly about finishing their breakfasts. There was no discussion as to why I felt the way I did. No mention of the article again . . . ever. I went up to my room and cried. The Monday morning congratulations from my friends and teachers were wasted. My parents were right; there was nothing for me to be proud of. All that was left was shame. I had embarrassed myself and my parents.

CHAPTER 15

COLLEGE YEARS

I took my high school studies very seriously, and it paid off. I was accepted early decision at Vassar College, a proud member of the class of 1980. I arrived at the end of August, on a sweltering day, free of loans and driving my parents' old red-and-white Cadillac Sedan de Ville. My parents and sister took another car. They helped me unload my stuff, and then my mom loudly complained, "I can't take the heat, Lisa. I have to get out of here." And they left with a quick kiss and a wave.

I wanted them to help me set up my room and take me out to dinner like so many of the other families, but they didn't. I sat down on my bed in the stifling hot room and planned my next move. I declined to have dinner with my roommate, Jody Friedlander, and her family.

The first airless night in our dorm room was particularly harrowing. Jody and I lay in our beds on either side of the partition unit and tried to sleep, but the heat and the mosquitoes were relentless. I tried not to cry, but all I could think about was how much I missed Teddy and my parents. In that order. Hearing Jody tossing and turning, I finally said, "Are you up?"

"Yeah," she responded. "I'm miserable. How about you?"

"The same. Let's get out of here. I've got the car outside. I'll drop you off at your house first [in Brooklyn], and then I'll drive home to the Island. I don't like it here."

"Sounds good," she said.

I don't know what happened next. Perhaps it was the comfort of just knowing that we could leave that kept us in our beds and saw us through to the morning.

***

Despite having spent lots of time away from home in the past, I found it difficult to adjust to the first several weeks at school. Three days into the college thing and I was still crying. I asked my parents to please come up to Poughkeepsie for a quick dinner. As anticipated, my mother came up with a million reasons why she couldn't make the two-and-a-half-hour trip to see me, but my father came, with a gift of a paper bag filled with assorted bagels. We talked over a steak and baked potato dinner, and he told me how proud he was of me. He reassured me, as he would so many times in my life, that everything was going to be fine.

My dad. Calming, patient, and loving. I cried. I didn't want him to leave. I felt like a child on the first day of kindergarten, seeking safety in the strength of her parents' arms. He didn't try to teach me any lessons on being strong and tough. He just listened. He dropped me off at my dorm and drove back home. I was more than fine after that.

My dorm housed a mélange of students, none of whom I thought I'd ever have anything in common with:

• The hippie types in their scruffy jeans with long, untamed hair who openly smoked pot and played Frisbee in the grassy area in front of the dorm. I couldn't relate.

- The foreign elites who arrived in private planes and chauffeured limos carrying designer luggage filled with designer clothes (they always had their collars turned up) and who had vacation homes around the world. I couldn't relate.
- The preppy boarding school crowd who wore Top-Siders, lots of green and pink (also sported turned-up collars), and loose khaki pants or kilt-style skirts. They had cocktail parties and tailgate parties and mothers and grandmothers who were alumnae of Vassar. I couldn't relate.

Despite my initial fears and hesitations, I was fortunate to find my own eclectic group within the first week on campus. There was Lourdes, a Cuban-born beauty raised in an idyllic lifestyle in Panama, who arrived at school a carefully chaperoned virgin but who adapted quickly to the liberal ways of college life. She studied French and fashion. Lourdes graduated college as an Episcopalian but later converted to Judaism, married and divorced a Jewish doctor, and traced her Jewish ancestry back to a famous rabbi in Spain. She taught me the importance of involvement in the Jewish philanthropy world and the beauty of Shabbat. We now live in the same condominium complex in Coconut Grove, Florida.

Lenore, a pretty, smart, bubbly, and very determined girl of Italian descent whose aspirations were far above her middle-class Long Island upbringing. She was an English major who very successfully followed her sister to Wall Street and the lucrative financial world of New York City in the early 1980s.

Phyllis, a short, blonde, brilliant Episcopalian girl, was from a modest family on Cape Cod. She majored in Russian studies and played the cello.

Me, a serious but funny Long Island JAP (Jewish American Princess) who teetered around the cobblestones and mud of campus in high heels and tight jeans, a style that I picked up after having spent parts of each summer in Italy. I wore makeup to class and carried a pocketbook. I was a rare duck.

We were Vassar girls, each bringing something unique to the friendship circle. During sophomore year I declared myself a political science major with a vague goal of going to law school. I immersed myself in my schoolwork with an obsessive determination to do well. I'd start working on my assignments on the day that they were given, successfully escaping the dreaded all-nighter. I would have a leisurely dinner with my friends and then go back to my room to study. When the noise in the hall from various stereos and impromptu soccer games got too loud, I cloistered myself away in the library or a windowless room in the dorm basement. I could work only in quiet. I was usually in bed by eleven p.m., just as things in the dorm were heating up. My disciplined schedule helped me deal with my relentless anxiety.

***

I had daily telephone conversations with my mother, each of us needing someone with whom to complain. She would go into detail about all the problems that she was having with my father and my sister. I would frequently get off the phone so deeply depressed that I was unable to do my schoolwork. I countered with details about my social life, my school workload, or my anxiety of the moment. My mother and I had started the beginning of an unhealthy, codependent relationship that was to play itself out for decades.

We did manage to balance the gloom and doom by sharing amusing experiences that punctuated our days.

A giant ant infestation at my parents' home kept my mother in terror for several days until the exterminator was able to work his magic. Her fear was that the "crawling raisins" would march into her bed, into her pajamas, and ultimately into her warm private parts. In self-defense, she resorted to using rubber bands to secure the legs and arms of her pajamas. Somewhere into her second REM cycle, her numb appendages awakened her. She spent the rest of the night scratching and vigilant.

There was also the problem of my mother keeping track of her false eyelashes, which she wore religiously back then. The spidery little suckers would turn up in the most unusual places! One morning as she threw back the blankets to get up from bed, she noticed an eyelash stuck to my father's tush as he slept naked with his back turned from her. She triumphantly plucked it off, saying out loud, "Aha! There you are. I've been looking all over for you!" The image haunted me for days!

Then there was the report of my father's road rage incident that occurred one evening on the corner of Central Park South and Seventh Avenue in New York City. A man in a car behind my father's laid on his horn and was screaming curses at him through his open window because my father (no doubt preoccupied with his sports scores) was going too slowly and made them both miss the green light. My father stormed out of the car (he probably was getting bad scores) to have words with the guy. When the honker saw the size of my dad and the wild look in his eyes, he rolled up his window and tried to maneuver his car through the intersection. But his fear didn't last long. He shouted to my father through his half-open window (just in case), "Hey, asshole! Look, your car is rolling into the intersection! You big idiot! Look at your car, ha ha! Too bad, there go your glasses too!"

In my father's haste, he neglected to put the car in park, and sure enough, the Caddy was slowly rolling down the street. As for his glasses, they had fallen off in the heat of the moment and had gotten run over by a passing car. My mother really liked that story.

The ongoing drama between my father and the shy, young Polish cleaning woman was perhaps the most pathetic story. My mother liked Kasia, but my father disliked her for no apparent reason. He blamed the poor thing for everything!

"Janet, where are my new pants? I can't find them! They were right on my chair by the bed on Monday. *She* moved them! I know she did!"

"Janet, what happened to the money I left on the dresser last night? It's gone. She took it! I know she did!"

"Janet, my new bonsai tree is dying! Do you know how much those things cost? She overwatered it! I told her not to touch it! She touched it! I know she did!"

One morning he started in with her yet again, and she locked herself in my mother's walk-in bedroom closet, refusing to come out until *he* left the house. My mother tried to coax her, "Kasia, please stop crying and come out now. I promise he'll leave you alone. He's getting ready to leave now. Come out. We'll go downstairs and have a cup of tea."

My father took an exceptionally long time to get himself ready to leave the house that morning. When the car finally pulled out of the driveway, my mother assured Kasia that the coast was clear. She slowly emerged from the closet.

That was the last day that she worked at the Novick house. Another one bit the dust.

I could not imagine any of my friends having the same type of telephone conversations with their mother.

***

In my sophomore year at Vassar, I took a class on the Old Testament with professor Deborah Dash Moore, which jump-started my adult interest in my Jewish self. I spent my junior year at Amherst College, where I chaired a fund-raising campaign for the United Jewish Appeal among the limited number of Jewish students on campus. During the summer of 1979, I was chosen to join an American Zionist Youth Organization tour to Israel as a campus activist. I was embarrassingly out of my league on this trip, working with students intensely active in Jewish affairs and general advocacy efforts. The experience left a strong mark on me. I wanted what these future leaders of their Jewish communities had, a strong connection and commitment to our very rich Jewish heritage, its history, religion, culture, and diverse politics.

As soon as I got my first home, I began to host Sabbath and holiday dinners for both my family and Jewish and non-Jewish friends. We shared the story of the exodus during Passover, dipped apples in honey during the Jewish New Year of Rosh Hashanah, and lit candles on the menorah during Hanukkah. I wanted to engage in the beautiful traditions that I felt I had been denied as a child.

In 2004, while shopping in the Korean grocery store near my home in Ardsley, New York, I saw a sign to join the Chabad of the Dobbs Ferry's Women's Club for a trip to Crown Heights, Brooklyn. Chabad is the outreach group for the Lubavitchers, a Hasidic sect of Jews, whose spiritual and physical headquarters is in Crown Heights, the neighborhood where I lived in Brooklyn as a child. The Lubavitchers are the religious Jews whom I always questioned my grandmother about on our walks to Eastern Parkway. I knew the visit would be like stepping back in time; I would get the opportunity to drive through the streets that I left in 1965 and would finally learn, firsthand, about the community that I had been so curious about as a child. The visit and my subsequent involvement in Chabad filled the piece of me that I had long been missing.

***

When I was home from college, I saw that my father's morning routine had gradually been getting longer and longer. It was a good three or four hours from the time he would don his threadbare bathrobe and pound down the stairs to the kitchen until he finally left the house for the day. First began the taking of the pills, a ritual that had grown along with Dad's age and weight. His sedentary lifestyle and gluttonous eating habits resulted in high cholesterol, hypertension, and diabetes, with an occasional bout of gout and kidney stones. A wide array of pills was carefully taken each morning, and my father did his best to be diligent and avoid poisoning himself! He would remove the pills from their bottles and lay them out in a long, colorful line to be consumed from right to left. The relatively simple system was foolproof until he got distracted by a phone call. When trying to multitask, the line of little pharmaceuticals often got upset, and pills went falling to the floor or were scattered throughout the clutter on the breakfast table. Tablets had been known to show up days later in his robe pocket, underneath the baseboard heating, in the Temp Tee cream cheese tub, and even stuck between his toes. The process would begin again from scratch.

Once the pills were taken, my father could get down to the serious business of making his breakfast. He complained that my mother never prepared the meal for him, but we all secretly knew that he preferred getting everything together just the way he wanted. First came the careful construction of his breakfast sandwich. The foundation consisted of a bagel or bialy; if a friend had not already delivered fresh goods that morning, Dad was forced to resort to his frozen stash. The plated bagel was placed, if possible, in the path of a ray of sunlight to provide a natural thawing method. Then the main attraction was chosen, be it lox, whitefish, a can of sardines, chinook salmon, herring in tomato sauce, or a dollop of tuna or egg salad. The cream cheese was taken from the fridge to adapt to room temperature, and the vegetable accompaniments, which were added to give a healthy edge to the meal, included sliced scallions, cucumbers cut in rounds, whole radishes to munch, and sliced tomatoes. When the components were ready, they were assembled into his sandwich. The most important meal of the day was washed down with a cup of percolated coffee with half-and-half, the *Daily News*, the *New York Post*, and the *New York Times.*

In addition to the breakfast blowout, the kitchen doubled as Dad's office. The kitchen table served as his desk. Piles of unopened mail, a magnifying glass, business cards, paper clips, and pens and pencils fought for space among the greasy napkins and bagel crumbs. His chair was next to the wall phone, which had a long, coiled cord that was forever tangled. Because the phone was mounted by one of his friends, any tug on the cord invariably led to the phone being pulled out of the wall. It would then hang limply by its exposed wires, drywall dust dotting the kitchen table and Dad's bathrobe until he could arrange for someone to come to fix it.

In the middle of this chaos was the yellow legal pad that Dad used to organize not only his daily and weekly tasks but everyone else's as well! I suspect list making was his way of organizing the whirl of things constantly going through his mind. I inherited this list-making obsession and was always playfully ridiculed by my friends. Dad's pad was organized into sections: those who owed him money and the amounts, things for various friends to do, and things for his workers to do. His greatest joy was to start the day by being able to cross off things from his list, a mark of accomplishment. My mother and I brought it to his attention that there was a conspicuous lack of tasks on the list designated for *him* to do!

Dad's response was "I am the chief! The leader!"

My mother replied, "Look, Big Chief Sitting Bullshit, wipe the cream cheese off your lips and get back to your executive duties!"

One morning, while perusing his pages and pages of entries, Dad found the following note (courtesy of my mother) at the bottom of the list:

THINGS FOR JOHN TO DO
1. Make another fucking list!

Added to the morning's activities was my father's half-hearted attempt to complete one of the newspaper's crossword puzzles. Kept his mind fresh. Unlike my mother, who could accurately complete, in pen, in a little over one hour, the *New York Times* Sunday puzzle, my father's puzzle skills were more on the level of the Monday *Daily News*.

One morning, shortly before he went into the hospital, my father proudly announced to my mother that he had finished the puzzle. Since he was a known puzzle cheater, she said, "Let me take a look at what you did there, John."

He passed her the paper, and she checked his work for errors. The word "croat" jumped out at her, which was my father's five-letter answer to "What frogs do."

"You are a piece of work, Johnny. What did you write here? What is this? Frogs don't *croat*, they *croak*!"

He responded, "Leave it alone, Janet! It fits! Just leave it alone."

On school vacations I spent a lot of time with my father. I loved to visit New York City and preferred to hitch a ride with him rather than take the Long Island Railroad. For the most part, I enjoyed our car trips together. The biggest draw for me was the unpredictability of being in his company. It was never a straight route into the city, and invariably there would always be multiple stops along the way that proved entertaining for me.

Once we finally made it out of the house, the car ride together began with Dad vomiting out complaints about my mother. He had usually saved up a semester's worth of crap to purge, and I was forced to listen. I had hoped that we might talk about me, what I was studying, and what my plans were for my future, but we would never get there. At first, I listened to his rantings with a sympathetic ear; I knew that my mother was difficult and that he needed to vent, but it wasn't long before I got annoyed with his self-absorbed ramblings.

"Dad," I said, "you make me really nervous every time I'm in the car with you and all we talk about is how much you can't take Mommy and how horrible things are between you and everyone at home."

"Who else can I talk to?" he responded. "She's crazy!"

"Can't you talk to your friends? Dad, you're putting too much on me. Every time I'm alone with you, all you do is complain and complain. Leave. Why don't you just leave? Or why don't you finally speak to someone, a therapist, someone who can give you some help?"

"I don't need help, she needs help. You don't want me to talk, I won't."

I just wanted to jump out of the car and scream, but no emotion ever lasted very long when I was with my father. We both had the ability to suddenly blow up and cool down within a very short period. The anger, guilt, and frustration that I am sure raged within us both was held down time after time. Until we were all willing to work on ourselves, everyone struggled to find an outlet.

***

One of our stops was usually at my father's office in Williamsburg, Brooklyn. My father was the president of New York Pretzel, the company that made the soft pretzels that were sold at vendors on the streets of New York and at the kiosks in sports venues including Madison Square Garden and Yankee Stadium. As a child, I enjoyed going to the bakery to watch the dough being twisted into a pretzel shape by giant steel arms, then boiled, baked, and packed for shipment. Any pretzels with a distorted shape or missing parts were called "cripples." The poor, doughy unfortunates were just as delicious but not retail-worthy. They were gladly given away to anyone who wanted to pick them up. Some of the best customers were hungry cops on late-night shifts who would stop by the bakery for a nosh.

The office had switched locations several times, but the employees surprisingly remained the same for many years. Perhaps they all suffered from Stockholm syndrome? No one ever knew exactly when my dad would arrive, but when he did, it was like a hurricane blowing through the office. Perhaps out of guilt for not spending enough time overseeing his business, he compensated by micromanaging the staff. When they heard my father coming through the door, they braced themselves for whatever mood accompanied him.

Fortunately, Dad was blessed to have a very nice group working for him, and despite the subprofessional atmosphere, they managed to get their jobs done.

Handsome, even-tempered Ronnie Orfinger kept the pretzel company afloat with the skills of a seasoned diplomat. Younger than my dad, Ron started working at the pretzel company as a truck driver and eventually became Dad's partner. He ran the day-to-day operations of the business, which gave my father the freedom to begin and usually end myriad other moneymaking projects. Ronnie was the voice of reason when my father could not or would not think through ideas. Never one to give compliments, my dad truly respected and appreciated him.

Millie, the elderly, spinsterly office assistant, was the least affected by his presence. She sat at her desk, shrouded in a cloud of cigarette smoke, and wouldn't look up from her work or her cheese sandwich unless it was absolutely necessary. She and my father shared an understanding of each other, which was displayed with obnoxious banter. If the mood was light, Millie might say in her raspy cigarette voice, "Hey, John, you're a pain in my ass, you know that, John?"

Sylvia was a short, boxy woman who handled the accounts. She was raised in an Orthodox Jewish family but was cast out when she married a Spanish man with a low-level job. She was also feisty (a prerequisite for keeping your sanity during working hours) and managed to hold her own when up against my dad. Always pleasant, she kept my father in line with a smile and a simple "Yes, John" or "No, John." He liked that.

Gracie, who was also in charge of accounts, was a Hispanic woman who learned from Sylvia the art of handling their boss. When Dad was out of control and Gracie looked helpless, Sylvia slyly gave her directives in Spanish.

Dennis, my father's son, also worked in the office. He handled the money that was picked up from the subway sites.

Then there was Irving, the bookkeeper. Overweight, bald, and bespectacled, Irving lacked the skills to manage my father, and so he was the tragic fellow who bore the brunt of his tirades. It was never a pretty thing to watch as Irving got blamed for everything. Poor Irving had the unfortunate job of handling my father's personal finances, which included paying all his personal bills. If there wasn't enough money in the bank account, it was Irving's fault. If my father had told him to do something but the result did not work out in my father's favor, it was Irving's fault. No matter how ludicrous the accusation, Irving sucked it up. Though it seemed that Irving forgave him daily, it was hard to tell if either homicidal or suicidal thoughts were lurking inside!

The office could have been a Harvard Business School study in how *not* to run a business.

One of the pretzel office locations was near a creek in an industrial area, which was a breeding ground for rats. My father had hired a specialist to try to prevent a problem within the office, but there was little that could be done to manage the infestation outside. It was late in the afternoon when my father went into the small office bathroom, which could barely accommodate his girth. First came muffled sounds from my father, and then, much to everyone's surprise, the door flew open and my father came scrambling out with his pants around his ankles. A rat had come up through the pipes and jumped out of the toilet . . . straight for my father! Once everyone realized that he was okay, the laughter was uncontrollable. The day went down in pretzel history as "the Day Johnny Laughed in the Office."

The company was later sold to the Makkos family for reasons that I could never understand.

***

The 1970s brought along a host of friends who may not have been new to my father but were new to me.

Joseph "Joey Carpets" Giovinco was a regular guest at the breakfast table. He was a good-looking guy by all standards: salt-and-pepper hair, nice body, dark skin. The Brooklyn Italian persona took form in his wardrobe of tracksuits for every season, gold chains, and his thick wiseguy accent. I always liked Joey because not only did he help my family with assorted errands, house repairs, and food deliveries, but he also had a good sense of humor.

I have heard two stories of how Joey Carpets got his nickname. The first comes from my mother, who says that Joey's mother owned a carpet store in the old neighborhood. When Joey was growing up, hoodlums looking to hide from the police were hidden by his mother in the carpet rolls stored throughout the store.

The other story claims that Joey Carpets's name refers to his oral sex prowess with numerous women. I have no trouble believing either of the sources for his nom de guerre.

Solomon "Solly Boxcars" Levine was one of the men who was a constant companion to my father in those crazy years. According to Wikipedia, boxcars, also known as midnight, is the outcome of rolling the dice in a game of craps and getting a six on each die. The pair of six pips resembles a pair of boxcars on a freight train. He was a hulking, raw-looking guy from Brooklyn with hands the size of Ping-Pong paddles and a goofy smile with straggly teeth that went in several different directions. My mother secretly nicknamed him "Snaggletooth." He stuck to my father's side like a rottweiler protecting his human.

I knew that he and my father spent most nights at "the club," a card gambling mill located on the second floor of a Bowery tenement.

My mom's and my all-time favorite "Daddy story" was the time that my parents and Boxcars and his wife were invited to a black-tie affair, and they needed to rent tuxedos for the occasion. They went to a place owned by a friend of a friend who fully outfitted them. The proud shoppers came back to my parents' house and, like teenage girls after a trip to the mall, donned their new outfits to show my mother. Solly was resplendent in a powder-blue tuxedo trimmed in navy with a huge bow tie and matching cummerbund. My dad sported the same number but in light beige with brown trim. The ruffled shirt, bow tie, and cummerbund made my father look like Dancing Bear from the *Captain Kangaroo* show. My mother was temporarily speechless, and then words of disbelief spilled forth.

"Are you kidding! You guys look like something from a strolling minstrel show! Johnny, beige? Beige!"

"Buttercream," he corrected her.

She continued, "You look like an elephant dressed in a tuxedo! Who sold you these costumes? I won't go anywhere with you dressed like that!"

Boxcars and my father were visibly hurt by her reaction.

"What do you know?" my father retorted. "The salesman told us that these are the latest spring colors!"

"Oh really?" she shot back. "Johnny, listen to me. You look like a fat Easter Bunny! That bow tie! That ruffled shirt! You have no neck as it is! You both look like schmucks! Take them back and get black tuxedos, not mint green, not lilac, just black!"

Boxcars eventually faded from the picture (as did so many others over the years), and I never knew what happened to him.

***

I spent my junior year at Amherst College as part of the Twelve-College Exchange Program. In April 1979 my parents drove up to Amherst to drop off my sister so that she could spend a few days with me. That night we went to a Passover seder at the campus alumni center, and my parents drove home. To save my folks the trouble of driving all the way back to Amherst to pick up my sister, I met them for dinner in Springfield, Massachusetts, at a restaurant called Ciro's.

Our dinner companion was a friend of my father's, Francesco "Skyball" Scibelli. Skyball had a criminal record dating back to 1932 that included arrests for extortion, keeping liquor for sale, and "gaming on the Lord's Day." He became the powerful regional boss of the Genovese family operation after his predecessor, "Big Nose Sam," died in 1983. Skyball and his brothers ran a very successful junket to Las Vegas until he was federally indicted for illegal gaming and convicted in the late 1980s.[17]

When my parents and sister pulled into the driveway of their house later that evening, my mother immediately noticed that the window shade in my bedroom was up, which was not how she had left it. My father ordered my mother and sister out of the car and into their neighbor's home. Their wonderful neighbors Jack and Miriam always seemed happy to help my eccentric parents, and my parents were always happy to make them happy! Since Jack is Israeli, my father assumed that he was trained in the Israeli Defense Force and would surely own a "piece." The weapon would qualify him to take charge of the home invasion situation before the police had to be notified (never mind that Jack was middle-aged and he suffered from a severe eye injury that left his sight greatly impaired). The two brave men entered the house, which, sure enough, had been robbed of cash and jewelry.

* * *

Following the robbery, my father acquired, from his friend Ritchie, a samurai sword sheathed in a blue velveteen case, complete with a tassel! Ritchie, a short, balding, kind of dim-witted-looking guy, owned one of those ubiquitous schlock shops that sells everything from luggage and foam Statue of Liberty crowns to "authentic" antique rugs, furniture, and other knickknacks. These are the shops whose windows are plastered with permanent banners advertising "Liquidation Sale—Going Out of Business."

---

17. "Frank 'Skyball' Scibelli," Mafia Wiki, last updated March 25, 2019, https://mafia.wikia.org/wiki/Frank_%22Skyball%22_Scibelli.

The store was in Manhattan in the West Fifties near Central Park South, a perfect spot to lure in naive tourists. The only occupants I ever saw in the shop were a ragtag bunch of men who looked as if they had been recruited from the Bowery for work as salesmen. Sotheby's it wasn't. The shop was one of my dad's stops, and I frequently babysat the car for him when there were no parking spots available in the vicinity.

I can't imagine that the samurai sword would have been very helpful in the event of a home invasion, as it was unwieldy, and my father was never trained as a feudal Japanese warrior. Besides, it was kept in his closest. Not only was the sword a rather unorthodox choice of weapons, but it also was responsible for nearly getting him killed!

My parents were asleep one night when they heard sounds downstairs and thought someone might be trying to break into the house. My father whispered to my mother to call the police, and then he got out of bed, naked, and grabbed the sword. He slowly walked around the upstairs rooms, sword raised, in search of an intruder. When he got to my room, he was relieved to hear the police car pulling up in front of our house. The police spotted a large, naked man brandishing a sword and walking back and forth in the window. They got out of their car, siren on, guns drawn, and through their speaker told the naked intruder to drop his weapon and put up his hands.

By then my mother ran downstairs, threw open the front door, and was screaming, "Don't shoot! That's my husband! Don't shoot!"

All the commotion had awoken the neighbors, who were accustomed to seeing or hearing all kinds of strange things coming from the Novick home.

Decades later, after my father had died and I was cleaning out the house in preparation for my mother's move down to Florida, the sword once again caused a problem. My mother had grown attached to the sword over the years and didn't want me to throw it away.

"What would you like me to do with it?" I asked her incredulously.

"It was Daddy's. Don't just throw it out; give it to someone," she said.

"Are you insane? Who would you like to offer it to? Got anyone specific in mind?" I countered.

"I guess you're right. I'll take it to Florida with me," she concluded.

"That's a great idea, Ma. You can hold it across your lap while I push you in the wheelchair to the plane. You might have a problem storing it in the overhead compartment, but I am sure the stewardess wouldn't mind holding it up front for you.

"And then when you get it to Florida, Ma, how is it going to look when you arrive at your new home at the Palace [an elegant independent-living facility] with a samurai sword? Shall I introduce you as my mother, an elderly ninja warrior?"

Once I finally convinced her to leave the weapon behind, I had to think of a way to get rid of the thing. I thought of googling "ways to dispose of a samurai sword in suburban USA." I certainly could not leave it by the curb with the other rejects! My luck, it would be taken, used in a crime, and then traced back to me! Once again, neighbor Jack came to the rescue. He clearly recognized what a find it was and gladly took the sword.

In addition to the sword, Ritchie had given my father several "valuable" gifts that included a Persian rug, a set of blue-and-white Chinese vases, a set of blue-and-white Chinese dishes with a matching tea set, a pair of ivory statuettes of a Chinese emperor and empress on a mahogany pedestal, and an intricately carved figurine of elephants walking over a bridge. Despite my father's claim that these items were of significant value, they were never cared for by my parents. By the time my mother gave them to me when she was moving from Long Island to Miami, the elephants were no longer attached to the bridge, nor did they walk in a single file linked trunk to tail. The emperor and empress had lost their ceremonial headgear, and the rug smelled musty and was littered with bug carcasses due to it being left in the unfinished basement.

I was in a real quandary when it came to my mom's move and the sale or transport of the ivory treasures. I had read online that there were very strict regulations regarding what can be done with ivory, and I certainly did not want to wind up in federal custody for trafficking illegal goods. I ultimately decided that seeking an appraisal for my most valuable heirlooms would be a good first step. I sent photos of the treasures to a reputable appraiser online and waited anxiously to find out by how much my net worth would be enhanced.

Not really to my surprise, my father's gems were worthless! The ivory goods were made of resin and were valued at approximately fifty dollars for the pair. I did my own investigation of the Chinese dishes and vases, and contrary to my father's claim that they were from the Ming dynasty, it turned out that they were probably from the basement of the Chinese supermarket on Canal Street in New York City's Chinatown! Nothing was ever as it was made out to be when it involved my father.

I gathered up the entire batch of gifts and left them curbside in a box for either garbage pickup or some schlemiel (unlucky guy) to take, all the while envisioning himself striking it rich after an appraisal on *Antiques Roadshow*!

CHAPTER 16

LAS VEGAS

Thanks to Hollywood movies, most people are aware of the mob's history of influence in Sin City. Crime families, who were denied ownership in hotels with gaming licenses, used Jewish front men like Genovese associates Meyer Lansky and Bugsy Siegel to gain access to casino profits. Remember Martin Scorsese's film *Casino* and Robert De Niro's character Sam "Ace" Rothstein, who was planted at the Vegas hotel by the Mafia to oversee the money-skimming racket? The movie was very accurate in its depiction of old Vegas.

In John L. Smith's unauthorized biography of Steve Wynn, *Running Scared: The Life and Treacherous Times of Las Vegas Casino King Steve Wynn*, Smith reported on the Genovese family's alleged strong ties with Mr. Wynn. He cites a confidential report by Scotland Yard that detailed the crime family's significant role in the rise of Wynn's Vegas empire. The report was prompted by Wynn's attempt to open a casino in London. Wynn was ultimately successful at having Smith's book removed from distribution following litigation. Although Wynn has denied any involvement with organized crime figures and has never been refused a gaming license, mob connections have been shown. In 1967, when he was twenty-five-years old, Steve Wynn started his empire in Las Vegas by purchasing a 3 percent interest in the Frontier Hotel. The Frontier was known to be controlled behind the scenes by the Detroit mob, while a crew of legitimate businessmen served as front men.

In April 1970 we went on our first family junket to Las Vegas and stayed at the Frontier Hotel. My father had already been there many times, and as a high roller, he was given VIP status. From the window of the plane, my father pointed out the strip, a blaze of lights in the middle of the dark desert. A limousine picked us up at what was then the small McCarran International Airport, and my father pointed out the sights along the way. He seemed happy to be with us. We were a family on vacation just like all the families I knew. I was thrilled.

During the summer and on college vacations between Christmas and New Year's, we took family vacations on junkets to the Dunes Hotel in Las Vegas led by Julius "Big Julie" Weintraub. Weintraub's nickname came from his six-foot-five, 230-pound stature, his reputation (beginning in 1959, he organized junkets from New York to Vegas that catered to high rollers), and his demeanor (he had a big heart and was happiest when pleasing his casino guests).

Julie was yet another good friend of my dad. Both had grown up alongside Mafia toughs to whom they had remained close throughout their lives. Julie's association with the Genovese family had once almost cost him his life and twice cost him his bid for a percentage ownership interest in the Dunes Hotel.

I had previously heard the story of Julie's problem with the mob, so it was not difficult for me to fill in the redacted parts in the following FBI files:

It is noted that . . . run "junkets" from New York City, to the Dunes Hotel, Las Vegas, Nevada. They have an office at . . .

> On June 11, 1968, . . . advised that he heard
> that . . . who was beaten up and hospitalized
> by unknown assailants during the past winter,
> is now "connected" with an Italian hoodlum
> from Brooklyn, known only as "FUNZI" or
> "FUNZAWALA." . . . did not know if members
> of "FUNZI'S" group had given . . . the beating
> last winter.[18]

My mother told me that mob associates broke Julie's knees and that she and my father had gone to Doctors Hospital in New York City to visit him. She said that the mob would have killed him after the initial attack had my father not interceded. I can only assume that the attack had something to do with mob involvement in the hotel.

On the surface, it may appear that a junket is a free trip, but nothing could be further from the truth. These trips are a business, and they aren't designed for you to go home as winners. No matter how much you are comped in the gourmet restaurants, how many shows you see, or how lavish your room is, the casino has the odds. If you are realistic, you view the junket as a nice vacation that has costs just like any other vacation.

The experience began on the plane ride out to the Vegas strip. The limited number of first-class seats on the plane was reserved for the VIP high rollers, but to avoid an in-flight mutiny, Big Julie was smart enough to provide everyone with the same amenities. From the time the plane took off until landing, it was one loud, unruly party, complete with drinking, deli sandwich eating, and smoking. We learned that behind the scenes the flight crews did everything to avoid manning the junket flights. Not even the big tips that Julie gave out compensated for the hellish job of trying to manage people who felt entitled to make their own rules, not follow them. The

---

18. Federal Bureau of Investigation, field office file NY 92-2476.

junketeers didn't want to put on their seat belts when asked, they smoked in the aisles, they got drunk and sloppy, and they generously indulged themselves in the restrooms . . . drugs, sex . . . it was all part of the experience. Since Big Julie and his brother, Charlie, were also jewelers on Forty-Seventh Street in New York City, they got everyone into a spending mood by raffling off a piece of jewelry from their store. Across the aisles the conversation was almost the same:

"Harold, look at that watch! I gotta have that watch. Look how beautiful it looks on Julie's wife. Buy some raffle tickets."

"Milt, *Milt*, you promised to buy me a watch for my birthday. It'll be my birthday in a few months. Buy tickets. Buy lots of tickets!"

"Pauly, ya gotta get me that watch! Buy some raffle tickets. Buy a lot of raffle tickets. I love that watch. Look at the diamonds, Pauly. They're sparkling at me!"

The opulence and decadence were exemplified by the stretch limo that picked up the high rollers at the airport and whisked them off to the hotel; a bus took everyone else. Julie distributed the room keys in the ballroom where a nosh buffet was set up for the guests—food played a major role on these trips. There was always some argument over the rooms. Invariably, some new couple from Canarsie or Yonkers was unhappy with their standard room assignment, believing instead that their credit line made them suite-worthy. Julie and his much younger, always elegant wife, Barbara, handled these types of situations with the aplomb of a seasoned diplomat. It was no easy feat massaging seventy-five egos engorged with a sense of entitlement. Once my father was settled into the suite of his choice, it was time to go, go, go!

***

The days began with breakfast delivered to the room. If there were five of us, my dad ordered enough for ten people. He wanted a little bit of everything: lox eggs and onions, pancakes, fruit salad, oatmeal (for my mother), and an assortment of bagels, muffins, and Danish. The poor waiters who delivered our breakfast could count on at least two more trips back to the kitchen for hotter coffee, crisper toast, or more cream cheese. My father had a huge distended stomach (he looked like he was in his eighth month of pregnancy, popped belly button included), and doctors had warned him of the health risks of his gluttony. I would fight with him over these mini buffets, but he had an answer for everything.

"Just eat as much as you want. Mommy likes to pick at the food all day. These are fruit Danish; I'll just eat the fruit part. The doctor told me that I have to eat fruit."

During the winter trips, I kept busy by visiting other hotels, having long lunches, watching TV, or reading. In the summer, I'd hang out at the pool, cooking myself under the hot desert sun. The temperature could hit 110 degrees, but as I often heard from the locals, "It's not so bad, at least there's no humidity!"

The calmness of the strip during the daytime belied what the night was to hold. When the sun went down, thousands and thousands of lights were ignited in a blaze of color, people awoke from their naps, and they started to fill the streets with an energy fueled by anticipation and hope. Themed hotels such as the Dunes, the Aladdin, Caesars Palace, the Flamingo, the Sands, and Circus Circus wooed guests with their huge flashing signs and the promise of mystery and adventure within. Hotel marquees announced the names of world-class performers and nude showgirl revues, constant reminders to even the most jaded that Sin City was like no other. Over the years I had enjoyed ringside seats to see such greats as Cher, Liberace,

Paul Anka, the Osmonds, Wayne Newton, Shecky Greene, Don Rickles, and Diana Ross.

Our dinner reservations were usually late, around nine p.m., at the Dome of the Sea or the Sultan's Table. We would arrive at the restaurant and make our way past a long line of people waiting for tables, where we were met by an obsequious maître d' who knew that my dad was a VIP and expected to be treated like one. I remember feeling an odd mix of embarrassment and excitement as we were escorted to the best table in the room. I enjoyed the special attention, but I could not help but feel ashamed that we were totally undeserving of it. Was my father a skilled surgeon who saved lives? Or perhaps an Atticus Finch–like lawyer who represented the causes of the downtrodden? A scientist? Novelist? War veteran? Teacher? Clergyman? Or anyone else for that matter who had a positive impact on people's lives? And what was I, other than John Novick's daughter?

My confusion would fade after we were seated at the table and expensive champagne and fine wines were poured into a dizzying array of glasses arranged at our places. It should be noted that my parents and I were not drinkers; we took only a few sips of anything that was poured into a glass that had a stem. It was all about the entitlement, the "we can and so we will" mentality. We much preferred the cans of Dr. Brown's diet cream and cherry soda that also graced our table.

We never ate alone as a family; dinner was always with an entourage. Jackie Leonard, my dad's dear friend and the casino host at the Hilton, and his wife, Janey, would always have at least one dinner with us when we were in town. Our meals were long, schlepped-out, elegant eating fests. At the Dome of the Sea, we were serenaded by a woman dressed in a ball gown playing a harp, who was seated on a moving platform in a pond situated in the middle of the restaurant. At the Sultan's Table, we chowed down on huge platters of fresh seafood on ice, four-pound lobsters, beef Wellington, duck à l'orange, or giant steaks, to the strains of violin music. My dad ordered and ordered food he loved and even food he hated . . . simply because he could. He ordered dishes, took a taste, and declared them "too salty" or "too greasy" or "too bland" or "too rare" or "too overcooked." Desserts were spectacles in themselves, flaming meringue molds of Baked Alaska paraded out by a line of waiters, pastel-colored petit fours, aperitifs in every color and flavor, all complemented by cups of freshly brewed strong coffee to prepare each of us for the evening ahead.

I loved those meals together because for the most part everyone was on his or her best behavior. If my mother was in a good mood, so were we all. She was a glamorous charmer when she wanted to be, and in those times, everyone really enjoyed her company. Her specialty was making clever fun of my father and his odd ways, or *schticklach*. Those close to us readily joined in the fun. Those not so close were uncomfortable, not knowing whether to laugh in order to be polite or not laugh in order to be respectful to my father. Dad always took the joking well, especially since my mother was undeniably accurate in the content of her routines.

***

By the late 1970s my father was well known in Vegas as a big gambler. From what I heard, he and Benny were partners at craps and blackjack. Those were the only games my dad played, having declared that roulette and the slots were strictly for suckers. My mom was a good blackjack player but preferred to pump thousands of dollars into the slot machines. She could sit for hours at the same machine, slowly feeding it the maximum. Despite the odds against her, the sheer volume of her pulls guaranteed some level of a win. Two pathetic cherries in a row emitted a weak *ting ting* from the bandit while a straight line of gold bars set off a light-and-sound show guaranteed to draw a crowd. She had a good thing going with my father when it came to gambling. He would give her money to play to keep her busy. If she lost, he would have to freshen her money supply, but if she won, she kept the money. There was no payback; money flowed in only one direction! Nothing made her happier than a paper bucket full of filthy silver dollars just waiting to be cashed in at the cage.

On my trips to Vegas, my father introduced me to a host of interesting people. I met all types of sports figures and masters of the universe—businessmen and women who had grown up in Brooklyn with my dad and moved to Vegas in search of their fortunes. I met wiseguys from different crime families who held various ranks within their organizations. The more bizarre their stories, the more fascinated I was.

One of my favorite encounters occurred when my boyfriend Teddy joined us on a visit to Vegas. Joe DiMaggio, a friend of my dad's, and Father Joe, the Yankees' team priest, joined us on a junket to the Dunes. My father, in his infinite wisdom, decided that Father Joe would be a good roommate for Ted.

The next morning at breakfast, Ted told us about his long, sleepless night. Father Joe's snoring had kept Teddy tossing and turning for the four hours that the priest had trained himself to sleep. For the rest of the night, Father Joe was up reading and doing paperwork. What exactly was the purpose of Father's Joe's visit to Vegas?

After two nights, my parents took pity on poor Teddy and allowed him to stay on the pull-out sofa in the living room of my suite.

***

I found my father's friend Stu Ungar to be one of the most fascinating men of those I met in Vegas. I was introduced to Stuey in the early 1980s over lunch at the coffee shop in the Dunes Hotel. Prior to us meeting, my dad told me a little about his background.

Stuey, nicknamed "the Kid" because of his man-child appearance, was known as perhaps the greatest Texas Hold'em and gin rummy player of all time. My dad knew Stuey's father, Ido, from Brooklyn, where he had owned a bar and social club known for hosting underground card games. Stuey hung around the club as a child, and thanks to his prodigy-level IQ and photographic memory, he quickly made a name for himself in card-playing circles. He dropped out of school in the tenth grade to play cards full-time. He had a reputation for his arrogance at the tables, which made him unpopular with many of the other high-stakes players.[19] The guy I met was very nice, but something was obviously wrong with him. Stuey couldn't sit still for a second; he was a skinny ball of motion—tapping, squirming, and fast-talking.

I made plans to watch Stuey play in an upcoming poker tournament. My interest in him as a pro was misconstrued by my dad as possibly something more, and he lost no time in telling me not to get too friendly as Stuey had "a lot of problems." What a surprise. Everyone I met through my father had a lot of problems. The Kid was always in debt despite the millions he earned playing cards. He literally blew all his winnings on sports, gambling, and cocaine. The drug had done so much damage to his nose that it had collapsed into a stump that could barely support the large sunglasses he wore constantly in an attempt to hide his deformity. Crack use later replaced cocaine and hastened Stuey's demise. The only thing that separated him from the junkies on the streets of Vegas were the

---

19. Wikipedia, s.v. "Stu Ungar," last modified July 30, 2019, 15:23, https://en.wikipedia.org/wiki/Stu_Ungar.

large stacks of poker chips that enabled him to feed his lethal habit.

In 1998 I read in the papers that Stuey, at age forty-five, was found dead from heart failure caused by his drug addiction in the Oasis Motel in Vegas. He was alone and broke at the time of his death. He left behind a teenage daughter from his ex-wife.

While researching Stuey, I learned that he had a history of connection to the Genovese crime family. I had assumed that his friendship with my dad was based on his addiction to sports betting, but apparently there was more. Stuey's in with the family started with his relationship with Victor Romano, a card-playing genius and a reputed street soldier in the Genovese family. Romano quickly became Stuey's mentor and protector. Some protector.

***

On a New Year's junket to Las Vegas in the late 1970s, Douglas LaChance and his wife were part of my father's entourage. It was the first time that I had met Doug, who was introduced to me as the president of the Newspaper and Mail Deliverers' Union (NMDU). The 1,600-member union, which represented workers at powerhouses such as the *New York Times*, the *New York Post*, the *Daily News*, and the *Wall Street Journal*, wielded enormous power, as "it controlled the only way the newspaper companies could get daily papers to readers quickly."[20]

The mob's lucrative infiltration of the NMDU spanned decades. The spoils, which were shared between the five families in the New York metropolitan area, were derived from a variety of tactics, including extortion from wholesalers in return for the promise of union stability and signed contracts,

---

20. Douglas Martin, "Douglas LaChance, Who Led Newspapers Deliveries' Union, Dies at 69," *New York Times*, September 26, 2011.

the sale of stolen newspapers, and loan-sharking and gambling among the drivers.[21]

Doug LaChance was known to have strong connections to the Lucchese crime family. His first elected term as president of the NMDU was from 1976 to 1980. In May 1980 he was indicted on 124 counts of extortion, racketeering, and income tax evasion. He received a twelve-year sentence but served only five years. He served a second term as president of the union from 1991 to 1993. Manhattan district attorney Robert Morgenthau, who conducted a three-year investigation of mob influence in the union, brought a case against LaChance, which led to an acquittal. LaChance served another short stint in prison for testing positive for cocaine use, a violation of his parole. He resigned from his position with the NMDU in 1993.

Our Vegas trip was the first and last time that I ever saw or heard my father mention Doug and his wife. In 2011 LaChance died from a heart attack at the age of sixty-nine.

＊

Irving Bitz, also known as "the Little Guy," whom I never had the "pleasure" of meeting, was the owner of a newspaper delivery company and had strong mob ties and an extensive criminal record dating back to the 1920s. He was the prime suspect in the murder of Legs Diamond, a notorious bootlegger, and was also the go-between with the mob and the FBI during the Lindbergh kidnapping investigation. In 1959 Bitz was convicted of labor racketeering, having forced newspapers in his district to use his services or risk labor unrest.

I was surprised to learn from my research that during the 1970s Bitz was a close associate of Funzi Tieri. He and the

---

21. Tom Robbins, "The Newspaper Racket," *Village Voice*, March 6, 2001.

Genovese crime boss reportedly had breakfast together every morning.[22]

In September 1981 the body of seventy-eight-year-old Bitz was found washed up on a beach in Staten Island. He had been strangled, and his death was ruled a gangland murder.[23]

In those days, it never crossed my mind how my dad met all these guys from such diverse backgrounds. I now realize they all shared a common thread, the Genovese family.

***

The last day of a Vegas junket always lacked the upbeat, electric atmosphere of our arrival. Most of the gamblers had neither left the hotel nor seen sunlight or a clock since they entered the Dunes Hotel five days prior. Gone was their collective vim and vigor. The group was sullen, overcome with a gray pallor and looking as if they hadn't changed their clothes in days. Pockets of cash had been replaced by pockets full of casino markers. The late nights at the tables and the stress of the play had left even the loudest and most obnoxious junketeers exhausted, irritable, and somewhat humbled. All that remained was a bunch of wrung-out men and women who had lost their money and gained at least ten pounds from the food orgies—souvenirs that would last longer than any T-shirt or postcard. Lady Luck had left the premises.

My mom and I still remember an incident that exemplified the testiness of the atmosphere on the last day of a junket. We were getting ready to leave for the airport, and everyone was passing the time in the coffee shop, filling up on one last cup of coffee and wrapping up multiple pieces of cheese Danish—a New Yorker's answer to survival food should the plane go

---

22. Robbins, "The Newspaper Racket."
23. Jim Mulvaney, "Racketeer's Body Found," *Daily News*, September 24, 1981.

down in the desert or, more likely, a travel delay lasting a few hours. There was an announcement that the transportation to the airport would be arriving soon and the travelers should claim their coats and carry-on luggage from the valet's desk in the casino lobby. There was a mad rush from the junketeers to get their stuff; everyone wanted to be first in the nonexistent line. Any shred of politeness that might have existed earlier in the week was gone . . . it was the running of the bulls, Las Vegas style!

A short, slightly built, older man with big, thick-lensed glasses pushed me in his haste to get to the front of the line. I fell off a small step leading up to the desk where a frightened woman had the job of collecting everyone's claim tickets. My father, who was outside the crowd, saw what had happened and ran over to help me up. The octogenarian offered neither help nor an apology, which did not sit well with my dad.

"What's the rush?" my father said. "Where are you going? You pushed my daughter down the step."

"Who the hell are you?" the old man responded. "You think you're a tough guy? You looking for a fight? I'll fight you!" He raised two little shaking fists in my father's face.

The crowd parted, and the spectators waited to see what would happen next. I looked at my father, who was like a bull that had just had the red cloth waved in front of him (albeit by a scrawny old matador), and I knew what was next. "No, Daddy, come on, let's just step away. I'm okay, really. Let's just go." And we did.

The end of a junket usually brought the worst out in people, no matter their age.

Big Julie spent his time on the plane trip back to New York settling his guests' accounts. Money lost in the casinos had to be paid back. The flight home was considerably less rowdy than the outbound segment.

CHAPTER 17

THE EARLY 1980s

I graduated from Vassar in May 1980, was elected to Phi Beta Kappa, and started a two- year master's degree program at Columbia University's School of International and Public Affairs in September. My father was disappointed that I had decided against going to law school; he was rightly concerned about what I planned to do with a future degree in international affairs, as I didn't have a clue. I was fiercely focused on my schoolwork and got good grades but was unable to translate it all into a career goal.

The obvious part of the problem was that I was spoiled; I had the luxury of not having to pay for my own education, and I took advantage of the opportunity to continue learning about subjects that fascinated me. Going to grad school was also a way of delaying finding a job and proving that I was more than just a high GPA. I was living in a deluxe building in Fort Lee, New Jersey, in a duplex apartment with a thirty-foot terrace facing the Hudson River that my father had bought from a friend at a very low price. I drove to Columbia every day in the Toyota Celica that my parents had bought me and was given enough money to enjoy all that New York City had to offer.

But my issues were much more complicated than just being overindulged. I had waited so long to be free from my parents' home, but oddly enough, when the time came, I was unable to detach from them and begin my adult life. Instead of fulfilling my dream of escaping the toxic environment of constant anxiety, fear, and uncertainty, I could not separate myself from it. I loved and hated my mother and father with such intensity and was so intermeshed in their dysfunctional lives that I was unable to concentrate on my own life. I felt disloyal if I was not available to listen to each of them complain about the other. I had my specific role in our family mess, and there was a sick comfort in its predictability and safety. By focusing on their problems, I didn't have to deal with my own. I could blame, I could procrastinate, and I could prolong my childhood, no matter how unhappy it had been. The whole family was a code-pendent mess that clung together for dear life. We each self-ishly took what we needed from one another regardless of the cost, and we all suffered greatly.

I lived my life in a heightened state of different emotions, often creating a level of crisis for things that were not warranted. I loved my classes but approached my studies with a seriousness that belied the fact that I was completely unsure of what I was going to do with my expensive advanced degree. I enjoyed the New York City single life but blamed every dud date on my own flaws rather than the man's or even our suitability. I had little respect for what is commonly today known as the "the journey." I was constantly running to get somewhere . . . I just didn't know where!

***

Not surprisingly, given my father-daughter issues, one of the biggest challenges in my life concerned men and my choice of them. Intellectually, I understood that the best shot at a successful relationship entailed commonality in values, religion, socioeconomic background, and level of education. Most of my girlfriends grew up hearing this from their parents and, as a result, were selective in their dating choices. I was not. My parents never guided me down the dating aisle, and I most certainly did not possess a natural ability to select the best candidate for the task at hand. I had been exposed to all types of men and found something appealing in many of them, no matter how unsuitable they were for me.

I dated a sampling of some of the most attractive and interesting men that the world had to offer. There was Alejandro from Argentina, Carlos from Portugal, Mohammad from Morocco, Bijan from Iran, Ofer from Israel, Massimo from Italy, Peter from Greece, and James from England. Stateside, I explored men in law enforcement and the military, wealthy Wall Streeters, cowboys from the heartland, the grandson of a famous Madison Avenue art gallery owner, a southern gentleman, and even a couple of *Saturday Night Fever* types! I believed, on some crazy level, that I could make a life with almost all of them, as long as they were smart and reasonably attractive. I could prod the lazy ones into success and the quiet ones out of their shell; the not-so-nice ones could be turned around with the power of love, and the wayward ones could be taught to walk a straight line. All of them could be taught to speak English. I fancied myself as Oprah, Sister Sarah from *Guys and Dolls*, Dr. Phil, and God—all rolled into a neat, tall, and toothy package.

My sporadic interest in men was consistent with the lack of focus I had in almost every aspect of my life. I was delaying making tough life choices. Perhaps the best (or worst) example of this was my relationship with Dominic.

In the winter of 1980, I was twenty-two years old and in my first year of graduate school at Columbia. On December 11, 1980, my dad had invited me to join him and my mom at

a popular Midtown restaurant called Nanni Il Valletto. I hesi-
tated to say yes, as I had to finish a final paper for the semester,
but my father insisted. "Come on, you'll have a nice time," he
said. "The food's supposed to be good at this place. That guy
from Harry M. Stevens is coming too; you'll meet him. Come
with Mommy and me. It'll be a nice evening."

It was a bitter cold night, and I wore my silver coyote coat
over a gray wool suit with a black turtleneck. My long, shapely
legs were accentuated by black stockings and black high-heeled
pumps. My waist-length, thick dark brown hair was tied up in
a high ponytail with a black ribbon, my signature hairstyle. I
was seated in between my mom and Dominic, whom I had met
a couple of weeks prior while attending the Sugar Ray Leonard
vs. Roberto Durán II (a.k.a. "No Más Fight") at Madison Square
Garden with my dad and my date. Dominic was the vice president of labor relations for Harry M. Stevens Corporation, a
privately owned company that owned the concessions stands
that catered to the sporting world. HMS clients included Shea
Stadium and Madison Square Garden in New York and the
Meadowlands Racetrack in New Jersey. My father's company,
New York Pretzel, provided the large soft pretzels to these venues via HMS.

Dominic was tall and solidly built, with thick, carefully
coiffed hair; a great smile; and a terrific sense of humor. He
wore tailored suits, a cashmere coat, highly polished shoes,
cuff links and had manicured nails. Think John Gotti. He
oozed confidence with a smattering of arrogance, and I could
see instantly why he and my dad were associated on both a
business and personal level.

Dom and I spent the evening talking, and toward the
end of the meal, he asked if he could take me to dinner and a
Broadway show that Saturday night. I had enjoyed our conversation and the attention, but a date? My mind was racing. He
was forty-four years old, and I was twenty-two! He had a son

my age! He wasn't even divorced from his wife; they were just recently separated! He was an important business partner of my father's, and I had heard something about never mixing business with pleasure.

There was another little complication. I had recently started dating a brilliant, tall, nice-looking Jewish boy from New Jersey who was a student at Columbia Law School. He was, by all standards, a real catch. I liked him but feared that he might be a bit too square for me and my family, or rather my family and I might be a bit too rough for him. These were reasons for our breakup that I felt I could never truly share with him. After a little more than one month, he declared his intentions by inviting me to meet his mom, dad, and sister for drinks at the top of the World Trade Center. The family was lovely, so normal and respectful of one another. The conversation was so intelligent—very PBS and Upper West Side Manhattan Jewish. His mother wore sensible shoes and carried a canvas tote from the Metropolitan Museum of Art. His father wore a bow tie and a fedora. We were doomed.

It was no surprise to me, when, with my mother's approval, I accepted a date with Dominic. After dinner, my parents went home, and Dom and I went to the Fort Lee Diner to continue to get to know one another until four a.m. Neither I nor my mother told my father about the first date with Dom, knowing that he would not be happy with the match. When my dad did find out, he was furious! He blamed me first for not telling him, but he saved the bulk of his anger for condemnation of Dominic's behavior.

"I invite him to dinner and this is what he does? He has the nerve to ask you out without even coming to me first? It's wrong, Lisa. He had no business doing that. It shows no respect for me, and he knows he didn't do the right thing! He's not for you! I don't want you to go with him."

My dad knew Dom as a ladies' man with some drinking and gambling issues. Prior to dating me (daughter of the pretzel vendor), he was involved with the daughter of the ice cream vendor. Who would be next, the hot dog progeny? I understood my dad's thinking, even the old-world Mafia respect thing, and I cared, I really did. I didn't want to defy my dad, but clearly something very psychological was playing itself out in this dance. I think that in going with Dom, I had entered a somewhat cleaned-up version of my father's world. Dom knew all about my father's associations, so there was no need to explain, no shock or risk of rejection. I was living the life that I had been accustomed to as Johnny Novick's daughter, only now, I was Dominic's girlfriend. I was a student by day, and at night I dressed up for dinners at Romeo Salta, got VIP treatment at the Meadowlands, accompanied him on business trips, and received grown-up jewelry gifts. A very misguided ideal of having arrived.

In February 1981 Dom took me with him to the National Labor and Management Conference at the Diplomat Hotel in Hollywood, Florida. We had dinner one night along with many of the conference executives at Christine Lee's restaurant, which was then at the Thunderbird Motel in Sunny Isles. Dom was taking me around to the different tables introducing me to everyone. A distinguished gray-haired man stood up to shake my hand, and Dominic said to him, "This is Lisa Novick, Johnny Novick's daughter."

The man, Vito Pitta, was the president of the New York Hotel and Motel Trades Council and held a powerful position as chief executive of the 25,000-member Local 6 of the Hotel, Motel, and Club Employees Union. He was also a reputed associate of the Columbo family. In October 1984 Mr. Pitta and eleven Columbo family leaders were hit with a fifty-one-count federal indictment. He was accused of using "force, violence and fear" to extort money from restaurants in return for labor peace.[24] In 1986 the President's Commission on Organized Crime issued a report to the president and the attorney general entitled *The Edge: Organized Crime, Business, and Labor Unions*. Law enforcement found that of the thousands of restaurants in the city, only several hundreds were unionized. No surprise there, as the mob, via the unions, controlled how restaurants did their business in New York City. In 1995 Mr. Pitta retired from the union, and in 1998 he retired from the council.

Mr. Pitta slapped Dom on the back and said to me, "Please send your dad my regards."

I nodded and got instantly nervous. I knew that my father would not have been happy that I was being paraded around. I was where I didn't belong.

Dominic and I continued together for six difficult months, and then we split, each wanting a relationship with someone more age appropriate. During the time that we had dated, my dad refused to have anything to do with Dominic; Ronnie, his partner, handled their business dealings. My father and I continued our relationship, but we never mentioned Dom. Just as soon as I told Dad that Dom and I were over, he resumed their business and personal relationship as if nothing had ever happened. In retrospect, I admire my dad's patience and restraint; he was smart enough to let things die a natural death.

---

24. Arnold H. Lubasch, "11 Indicted by U.S. as the Leadership of a Crime Family," *New York Times*, October 25, 1984.

CHAPTER 18

SOME FRIENDS

During my years in grad school, Dad and I spent a lot of time together. He was always in the city, and I would often meet him after my classes at one of his friend's offices. We'd have dinner with whichever of his friends didn't have to go home to their wife and kids.

I enjoyed being part of Dad's entourage. He seemed to be at the top of his game in those years, confident and capable. In addition to the usual flock of cuckoo birds whom he surrounded himself with, he was also close to a gaggle of successful businesspeople. Looking for an easy way in, I had hoped that through my father's connections, I could skip the arduous work of job searching and land a big job, perhaps a husband, or maybe both. As a result, I found it increasingly easy to make excuses for his past and present bad behavior no matter how much I disagreed with his ideas or actions. I certainly gave him more of a pass than I did my mother.

My father loved to be with people; he wasn't one who needed or liked to be alone. He didn't read books, didn't have hobbies other than sports watching and betting, didn't particularly enjoy family time . . . you get the picture. In order to be

surrounded by people (men) most of the day and evening, you
need to have a lot of "friends." You need to have a lot of different
kinds of friends, since they need to serve different purposes.
You need friends who are not busy with their families and can
be available to have dinner, friends who are free to meet at
unusual hours to have lunch, friends who can pick up at short
notice and go to Las Vegas or Atlantic City, friends whom you
do business with, friends who are there for you when you need
help or a shoulder to complain on, and friends who don't do
anything; they just are there so that you don't have to be alone.

From my perspective, my father had three basic groups of
friends who crossed back and forth over blurred lines based on
the times and necessity:

- Those who were associates of the mob and with whom
  he conducted business as a moneymaker
- Those who were there for him on a daily basis, were
  involved in our family life, and who truly loved him
  for who he was rather than what he could do for them
- Those who just hung on for the ride and who came in
  and out of his life as needed

Their stories are sprinkled throughout this book.

Let's start with the mob-associated friendships whose
deep roots went back decades. Venero "Benny Eggs" Mangano
was one of my father's closest friends. Benny was born in 1921
in Lower Manhattan. He acquired his nickname because his
mother owned an egg farm. Benny was a decorated member of
the US Army Air Corps, having served in Europe in World War
II as a bomber tail gunner. He later owned a surplus clothing
distribution business that bought overstock from customers
such as Calvin Klein. Barry Schwartz, Klein's business partner,
became a friend of my father and Benny.

At first, a friendship between my dad and Benny seemed highly unlikely: Novick, a tall, stocky Jew with Russian roots, and Mangano, a short, squat Italian. But both were highly intelligent, shrewd businessmen who respected each other for their individual strengths. Both were connected to the Genovese crime family, Benny as a "made man" and my father as a moneymaking facilitator.

My father would meet Benny several times a week in or near his apartment in the West Village. Dad never ate dinner with us during the week when I was growing up, but Benny was a family man and preferred to eat dinner at home or in his neighborhood. After dinner Benny usually would go out to do business at "the club" at 110 Thompson Street, in what is now fashionable SoHo. Before the art galleries, retail stores, and trendy restaurants began to spring up in the early 1980s, it was dark and desolate at night in the area south of Houston Street (how SoHo got its name). The club was on the bottom floor of a tenement built in 1900. Old Italian men would sit outside the door, no matter what the weather, on folding chairs while neighborhood kids played basketball on the courts in the small concrete park adjacent to the building. I would often go to the club with my father after one of our dinners together, but I never went inside. I would sit in the car, which was usually double-parked on the old narrow street, and wait for him to come out.

Remember photos from the mid-1980s of Vincent "the Chin" Gigante, the boss of the Genovese family, walking around the West Village in his bathrobe and slippers, unshaved and muttering to himself? While Gigante walked around the village like a patient out of *One Flew Over the Cuckoo's Nest*, allegedly Benny was his underboss, the second in command, overseeing the organization's daily operations.

My mother told me that when Gigante was in jail, it was my father who made the hotel arrangements for his wife and her guests whenever she wanted to go to Atlantic City. She also told me that one evening, just prior to Christmas, my parents pulled up outside the Triangle Social Club at 208 Sullivan Street. Gigante shuffled out in his sleepover attire, came over to the car, and through the open windows, wished my parents a merry Christmas, giving my mother a kiss.

***

Johnny "Johnny Sausage" or "Little Johnny" Barbato was another of my dad's closest friends. His nickname originated from his father's sausage store on Thompson Street in SoHo. To us, he was the Little Johnny (at five foot seven, about 170 pounds) to my father's Big John. He was always very kind to me and, in his soft-spoken voice, always took the time to ask about what was going on in my life. Johnny and his family lived in a modest home on Staten Island. None of my father's mob friends lived with the opulence that is often depicted on television. Johnny's older son was a super-nice guy, and he and I were friendly for a short period of time in the early 1980s. We had our fathers in common, a college education, and jobs in the shipping industry.

I was equally as fond of his attractive wife, Frances. With her two-toned black and platinum-blonde hair, heavy New York accent, street smarts, and razor-sharp wit, she looked like a character straight out of central casting for the movie *Married to the Mob*. I loved the time that I spent with them on weekend trips to Atlantic City. They were both merciless when it came to making fun of my father's eccentricities. Frances would lovingly refer to him as "the fat bastard," and Johnny was particularly fond of teasing him about his ageless dark hair.

According to Wikipedia, Johnny's ties to the Genovese family date back to the 1940s and the reign of Funzi Tieri.

He was later supposedly Benny's chauffeur and bodyguard.[25] Eventually, he was known to be a capo in the Genovese crime organization, with ties to Local 8 of the United Union of Roofers, Waterproofers, and Allied Workers in New York.[26]

My parents, the Manganos, and the Barbatos were always socializing together—a small circle of trusted friends who were comfortable in one another's company. The men shared business, and the women shared the fact that they were married to complicated men who had complicated lifestyles. For decades they traveled together to Vegas and Atlantic City for the casinos, Saratoga for the August races, and Miami for the relaxation.

My father considered Frank "Yay" Tramontano to also be one of his closest and most loyal friends. Yay has been described as a Bonanno crime family associate who ran the day-to-day operations of a mob-run gambling and loan-sharking ring. My mom says that he wasn't an associate of any family. I knew him as a baby-faced, easy-to-smile, family-oriented man.

Thanks to Yay, my friends and I had the opportunity on several occasions to eat at Rao's, the famous East Harlem Italian restaurant. Tables at the small restaurant are "owned," so even the rich and famous can only get access with a connection. Yay owned one of the coveted tables.

In August 2006 my father, Yay, and a few other men rented a house in Saratoga for the races. My daughter, Maggie, and I were invited to join them for a couple of nights, as I had always wanted to see the beautiful country racetrack. Unfortunately, my father's health had already started to decline, and he was able to attend the races only for one day. Maggie, my dad, Yay,

25. Wikipedia, s.v. "John Barbato," last modified June 30, 2019, 12:15, https://en.wikipedia.org/wiki/John_Barbato.
26. Thomas L. Lueck, "Roofing Union Charged With Scheme to Extort $2 Million," *New York Times*, July 28, 2004.

and the rest of their crew had dinner at the Wishing Well, the famous Saratoga eatery.

In 1984 my father sold the Fort Lee apartment to his friend Yay, who bought it for his daughter. My dad then bought me a one-bedroom co-op in the Brevard, at 245 East Fifty-Fourth Street in New York City. I was happy in my New York City days, not lonely as I had been while living in Jersey, where neither my friends nor family came to visit.

My first real memory of Murray Wilson, still another of Dad's close friends, goes back to 1983 when he was nice enough to hire me to work at his restaurant La Difference while I was between jobs. I wasn't a server or an event planner or a chef. What exactly I did for those several months evades me even now, but I do remember having had a very good time!

La Difference was a high-end, faux French, kosher restaurant located in the Roosevelt Hotel in Midtown Manhattan, near Grand Central Station. It catered to an observant, wealthy Jewish clientele who was willing to pay the exorbitant prices for otherwise so-so food. Wall Streeters in yarmulkes, bearded jewelers, and extended families from Borough Park gathered in the glitzy dining room to eat overpriced rib eye steaks and fish fillets that were purchased and prepared according to Jewish dietary laws.

The supervisor, or mashgiah, responsible for overseeing the kosher kitchen at La Difference was a tall, fat, bearded man who never looked up when he walked. He conducted most of his supervising while perched on a stool in the corner of the kitchen. To pass the time, he would read his newspaper, licking his chubby pointer finger to initiate each page turn. His "uniform" consisted of filthy white collared shirts whose buttons often lost the fight to prevent his equally dirty undershirt from making an appearance. The ill-fitting, grease-spotted black trousers all must have had defective fly zippers, as they were always partially open. His sensible black work shoes, the pleather dulled from layers of never-removed schmutz (crud), the untied laces dragging in the slop on the kitchen floor, completed his less-than-appetizing ensemble! For me, the most disturbing sight was the bits of food that were always nestled in his long, straggly beard. It was a good thing that he stayed in the kitchen when the restaurant was open to guests.

The maître d' was a Russian Jewish émigré named Greg. He had a big, bushy mustache; dressed very dapper; and had a nasally voice with what could have been mistaken for a French accent depending on one's level of sophistication. He answered the phone with a drawn-out "La Dee-fair-ance . . . may I help you?" To those who really wanted the French experience, one could squint and will themselves into believing that Greg was a haute Parisian rather than a Soviet transplant just a generation removed from a village like Anatevka in *Fiddler on the Roof.*

Greg was nice, capable, and eager to make his way in America. To help further his image, he bought my mother's 1979 navy-and-white Mark V Bill Blass Limited Edition Lincoln Continental, whose massive size and over-the-topness screamed excess. Nothing could have said "you've arrived" more than that behemoth! The sale made my mother happy; she had done her part to help with the integration of the Soviet Jews.

During Passover, a box of matzoh was placed on every table, in place of bread, which is forbidden during the holiday. One lunchtime, the staff and I sat down for a quick meal prior to the arrival of guests, and I reopened a box that contained a few leftover squares of the dry, unleavened bread. To our horror, we watched as a conga line of roaches made its way up and over the side of the box, onto the white tablecloth, and to safe refuge behind the red velvet banquettes. Several already opened boxes housed the same tenants, who also scattered to freedom once the roof of their temporary home was removed.

Our revulsion at one of nature's most resilient little creatures was met by uncontrollable laughter, the kind that grips you when the situation is more nerve prickling than funny.

***

I first saw a display of Murray's infamous temper one afternoon when he arrived at the restaurant. One of the staff members had done something that he shouldn't have, or maybe Murray had brought his anger in from outside. Whatever the case, he started screaming, got a wild look in his eyes, and overturned a table that had already been set for dinner. Scary.

Sammy Wattenstein and Zvi Hager were Orthodox Jews who were Murray's lackeys, usually at his side either to drive him around, run errands, or facilitate something business related. They were both schleppy-looking wannabe tough guys in their late twenties or early thirties who were neither smart nor ferocious. Both men overly inflated their own self-worth as a result of being in Murray's inner circle, despite being frequently verbally abused by Murray in public. Zvi, a rabbi's son, was clearly the more passive of the two clowns. Sammy was particularly pathetic, as he was fat with frizzy red hair, was always sloppily dressed, and had a lisp that caused him to spray saliva whenever he talked. I saw Sammy as an angry person, prone to cruelty in both word and deed at the slightest perceived provocation. In retrospect, he looked like an overweight Chucky doll in a yarmulke, including the bulging, crazy eyes but minus the bloody knife. Each personality in the unfortunate trifecta served a purpose.

Murray was a big supporter of Israel and had been very close with Rabbi Meir Kahane, the founder of Kach, the ultranationalist religious and political party in Israel, and the Jewish Defense League, a militant group in the United States dedicated to protecting Jews against anti-Semitism by whatever means necessary. Murray was also active in helping Russian Jewish émigrés resettle in Brooklyn. His involvement in the Russian community in Brighton Beach, Brooklyn, put him in the company of members of the powerful Russian mafia, which exploded in the 1980s as the USSR was delighted to empty its prisons and gift its criminals to the United States.

I never knew how or when my father and Murray became friends, but their involvement with the Genovese crime family was most probably the glue. I am told that it was my father who introduced Murray to Benny Eggs. Murray, who had made a reputation for himself as a skilled money launderer, was introduced to Evsei Agron, a ruthless Jewish Mafia boss. The Russian and Italian crime families saw in each other a way to expand their power, and it was Murray who arranged the blood marriage.[27]

In 1985 Murray and Sammy drove Zvi to the marshes of the Meadowlands in New Jersey, where he was roughed up, stripped of his clothes, and dumped by the turnpike. Why? Supposedly, Murray accused Zvi of attempting to break into his office.[28] To get revenge on the duo, Zvi went to the chief of security at the Dunes Hotel in Las Vegas and reported a moneymaking scheme that Murray had concocted in which he and Sammy had defrauded the hotel.

The government believed that it was Murray and his Russian Mafia pal Evsei Agron who were the brains behind the plan to relieve the Dunes Hotel of its money. Zvi alleged that in 1983 Murray had recommended people to be part of a junket to Vegas where they received credit, or markers, to gamble at the Dunes. Murray had admitted that Agron was one of the players for whom he had vouched as creditworthy. Markers allow the player to get casino chips with the understanding

---

27. United States v. Wilson, 924 F.2d 1064 (9th Cir. 1991).
28. William Bastone, "The Last Jewish Gangster," *Village Voice*, April 26, 1996.

that any winnings are to be used to repay the marker and losses are to be repaid promptly, by whatever means, upon returning home from the junkets. Murray arranged for junket guests to get their markers, gamble with a small amount, and then have the two stooges, Zvi and Sammy, take the balance of the chips and transfer them to another person, who would cash them in. The casino was then unable to trace the credit line where the chips should be applied.[29]

Recently over breakfast with my mom, I learned that the FBI had paid a visit to her home one morning, decades ago, to see if she could shed any light on this scheme. They knew that she had spent many hours in Murray Wilson's company at the Dunes casino. Over coffee and Danish at her kitchen table, they asked her about the Russians whom she had met at the Dunes, specifically if there appeared to be anything unusual about them at the blackjack tables where my mother often played. Mom told them that she knew nothing, and she phoned my father as soon as the FBI left. I would have fainted upon opening the door and seeing their badges (as would later be the case), but my mother was hardened to her lifestyle.

Zvi later refused to testify against Murray and, for some reason, was not forced to do so. However, the government had enough evidence without Zvi's testimony to find Murray guilty of defrauding the Dunes Hotel of more than $1 million. On June 30, 1989, he was sentenced to three years in the Federal Correctional Complex in Allenwood, Pennsylvania.

In the years after Murray got out of prison, he became successful with his New York City restaurants: Campagnola, on the Upper East Side, and Ecco, in the Financial District. He also successfully managed an Orthodox Jewish, Russian émigré fighter named Yuri Foreman. Foreman held the World

---

29. *United States*, 924 F.2d at 1064.

Boxing Association super welterweight title from 2009 to 2010. In 2014 he was ordained as a rabbi.[30]

Murray also became very close to Benny Eggs during the 1990s and early 2000s, a relationship that played a crucial role in the network of my father's friends.

When I moved into Manhattan, I gladly joined my parents for dinner at least once a week and truly enjoyed our time together, unless they happened to have one of their loud, ugly, public arguments. We frequently went to Elmer's, a restaurant across the street from my apartment on Second Avenue and owned by Albert "Albie" Goldstein.

Albie, a former marine and recipient of two Purple Hearts, was another of my father's good pals. Albie made a fortune as the owner of R-Jo Trucking, which was the sole distributor for the popular Key Food Cooperative Supermarket chain. It just so happened that Pasquale Conte, a capo in the Gambino family, sat on the board of directors of Key Food. Conte had served ten years in prison for racketeering charges and conspiracy to murder.

Albie and his wife, Joanie, were well known, well liked, and well connected on the New York social scene. Albie had met Joanie through her mother, whom he had dated for years. Mom out, Joanie in. They lived in the Sovereign, a luxury building in Manhattan, and had a driver named Red who transported them around town in their gold Rolls-Royce. Albie was a member of the prestigious Friars Club, famous for its celebrity roasts.

In the 1980s, Albie opened Elmer's steakhouse on Fifty-Fourth Street and Second Avenue, which was previously the legendary El Morocco club. From the 1930s through the 1950s, the nightclub had catered to New York's society crowd and a host of visiting movie stars and business magnates. By the time

---

30. Wikipedia, s.v. "Yuri Foreman," last modified June 18, 2019, 12:03, https://en.wikipedia.org/wiki/Yuri_Foreman.

Albie purchased El Morocco, it was left with only its illustrious history and its signature zebra-striped banquettes.

Albie had hoped to capitalize on the famous name by reinventing the club. In 1984 my father's good friend Charlie Meyerson, casino host for the Golden Nugget in Atlantic City, arranged to hold a party at Elmer's for the hotel's high rollers. The guests of honor were the hotel's owner, Steve Wynn, and the Goldsteins' old friend Frank Sinatra. Over three hundred guests took photos with their hosts, Sinatra, famed boxer Rocky Graziano, and Yankee great Roger Maris.

Elmer's didn't last long. In 1989 the federal government indicted Albie on fifty-eight counts of tax fraud and money laundering involving $10 million in undeclared earnings. He served eight months in the Allenwood Federal Correctional Complex. I never heard about him after that. Albie died in 2000 at age seventy-five.

CHAPTER 19

THE RECORD INDUSTRY

My father's connections to the record industry spanned decades, but it wasn't until the early 1980s that I learned about his involvement.

Morris Levy, who founded Roulette Records in 1956, was a friend of my father's whose office I visited many times. I loved looking at the photos and awards marking Levy's accomplishments and felt proud of my dad for knowing such a notable person.

It was not until the age of the internet that I began to do research on many of the men whom I had been introduced to by my father. I learned that Levy was known as the "Godfather of the Music Business," a title that he flaunted despite being connected to the mob.[31] Roulette Records was alleged to have been a front for Vincent "the Chin" Gigante and the Genovese family (thus the connection to my father) to launder mob money.

---

31. Richard Carlin, *Godfather of the Music Business: The Life and Times of Morris Levy* (Jackson: University Press of Mississippi, 2016).

Levy's specialty was cheating his artists out of their royalties using the tactic of claiming to have written the songs that he had only produced. He also used the strong-arm of the mob to threaten the lives of those artists who demanded the money that they were rightfully owed. What a guy!

Perhaps the most publicized example of Levy's treachery involved Tommy James and the Shondells, the group responsible for such blockbuster hits as "Hanky Panky," "Crimson and Clover," and "I Think We're Alone Now." In James's book, *Me, the Mob, and the Music: One Helluva Ride with Tommy James and the Shondells*, he details how Levy used his organized crime connections to swindle the group out of the money they were owed. James was so afraid of Levy and his associates that he waited until 2010, twenty years after Levy's death, before he released his book. James claims that Levy had cheated him out of approximately $30 million to $40 million in royalties.[32]

Levy was convicted on extortion charges in 1990 following an FBI investigation into the mob's influence in the record industry. He died that same year from liver cancer, just months before he was to begin his prison sentence.

Nat Tarnopol, another close friend of my father's, was the president of the R&B label Brunswick Records, a subsidiary label of Decca Records. He managed the careers of such greats as Barbara Acklin, Gene Chandler, the Artistics, Young-Holt Unlimited, Tyrone Davis, and the Chi-Lites.

Nat met singer and R&B legend Jackie Wilson in the late 1950s, as they were both from Detroit (or as my father used to say, "DEE-troit"). Under Tarnopol's direction, Brunswick Records catapulted Jackie Wilson to fame with such hits as "Lonely Teardrops," "That's Why (I Love You So)," "I'll Be Satisfied," "To Be Loved," and "Doggin' Around." In 1967,

---

32. Wikipedia, s.v. "Morris Levy," last modified July 26, 2019, 23:24, https://en.wikipedia.org/wiki/Morris_Levy.

Wilson also recorded the smash hit "(Your Love Keeps Lifting Me) Higher and Higher."

Prior to making his mark in the record industry, Nat had distinguished himself as a star baseball player. He was recruited to play with the Detroit Tigers and the Chicago White Sox.[33]

In the mid-1970s Tarnopol entertained the idea of buying the New York Yankees. He had been close friends with many of the Yankee players, including Reggie Jackson and Thurman Munson, and it was not uncommon for them to hang out at the Brunswick offices on Broadway. Through Nat, my dad became close to Munson and was invited to go for a plane ride with him just weeks prior to his fatal plane crash.

Between the music personalities, the sports figures, and his strong friendship with Nat, it was no wonder that my father loved to spend time at the Brunswick offices. I did too! In the early 1980s I would often meet my dad late in the afternoon at their headquarters on Broadway after my classes at Columbia University. Dad and I, and on occasion Nat, would go out to dinner on those evenings. I always enjoyed Nat's company; unlike some of my father's other friends, he was mild mannered and always a gentleman in my presence.

During my research, it became very clear how my father had come to know both Morris Levy and Nat. The mob was well entrenched in the record industry throughout the 1950s, 1960s, and 1970s. They demanded their cut on every aspect of the process of making a record, from coercing the signing of new talent, to making payolas (to corrupt DJs who refused to play records on the air until they received kickbacks), to cheating artists out of their royalties.

Nat had strong ties to the mob, particularly the Genovese family, most probably through my father. Gaetano "Corky" Vastola was a thug from New Jersey who had a long history

33. Wikipedia, s.v. "Nat Tarnopol," last modified July 18, 2019, 18:39, https://en.wikipedia.org/wiki/Nat_Tarnopol.

of criminal convictions. He was also a partner of Morris Levy in Roulette Records. It was alleged that Vastola controlled Tarnopol's relationship with Jackie Wilson, but I was unable to verify this. I did learn that around 1971 Jackie Wilson wanted to sever his management relationship with Nat. Despite Wilson's battle with drugs and alcohol, he blamed Tarnopol's mismanagement as the reason behind the decline of his career. Wilson, who was so fearful of Tarnopol's mob connections, decided to ask Vastola for help in ending the relationship.[34]

I had heard that it was my father who intervened between Vastola and Funzi Tieri and possibly saved Nat's life when the mob tried to strong-arm him. In the end, the management contract between Wilson and Tarnopol ended, and Tarnopol kept his life and Brunswick Records. I asked my mother about all of this. She said that she had never heard this story but wasn't at all surprised by the details.

"You see, Lisa," she said, "Daddy was very close to Funzi. They were very close. Daddy must've gone to Funzi with this situation, and that determined how things were handled."

In the mid-1970s the federal government conducted a probe of payola in the record industry. In 1975 Tarnopol and seven Brunswick executives, Clive Davis of Arista Records, Kenneth Gamble of Philadelphia International Records, and sixteen other independent record executives were charged with tax fraud and payola. In 1976 those indicted were found guilty.

In 1977 a US appellate court overturned the conviction of all the Brunswick executives. However, the judge's ruling indicated that there was enough evidence that Tarnopol and Brunswick Records had cheated their artists of their royalties. At that time, Wilson had the legal might, but had neither the health nor money to bring Brunswick to trial. In 1975 Wilson

---

34. Wikipedia, s.v. "Gaetano Vastola (gangster)," last modified February 5, 2019, 00:29, https://en.wikipedia.org/wiki/Gaetano_Vastola_(gangster).

suffered a massive heart attack on stage. He never saw his money and died in 1984.

The legal fees from the case left Brunswick Records without the resources needed to continue in the industry. I remember my father saying that Nat's legal troubles had left him a different person, angry and depressed. Dad always felt terribly for him and how his career had changed. Nat died of a heart attack in 1987 at age fifty-six.

It was Nat; his wife, June; and his son Paul who appeared in Diane Arbus's iconic 1968 photograph entitled *A Family on Their Lawn One Sunday in Westchester, New York.*

Another of the regulars at Nat's office was Al Sharpton. I didn't know if Sharpton worked at Brunswick, but I do remember that he was one of several guys who was always hanging out at the office, eager to get drinks and snacks for us at the market downstairs or put money in our parking meter.

Before his rise to fame, Sharpton was a large man with long, wavy hair. He dressed in jogging suits, which he adorned with thick gold chains and medallions around his neck. He was a far cry from today's gaunt TV and radio political commentator, who wears expensive, tailored suit and keeps company with President Obama.

It was widely reported that Sharpton had close contacts in the music and boxing industries, many of whom were tied to the mob in the New York City area. Beginning in the mid-1980s and spanning several years, Sharpton worked with the FBI and the NYPD as an informant, principally targeting the Genovese family. The information that Sharpton gathered was largely responsible for securing the green light from eight federal judges for signed wiretaps, including the office lines of Morris Levy. The evidence gathered eventually led to the conviction of key leaders in the Genovese hierarchy.

Carmine "Wassel" DeNoia was also part of the Brunswick Records entourage with whom my father associated. He was a perfect friend for my dad since he was unmarried and always available to hang out. I joined Wassel and my dad for dinner on several occasions, usually at the Stage Deli, where they both held court.

Wassel initially reminded me of Lennie in Steinbeck's *Of Mice and Men* (a large man with limited mental faculties), but I came to learn that he was anything but simple or slow. I found him to be a warm, funny, smart man with a very generous heart. One Christmas, he sent a photocard of himself dressed in his undershirt and pajama pants, with red suspenders and a hat. So festive! I enjoyed his company so much that in 1980 I convinced my mother to accept Wassel's invitation to Thanksgiving dinner at the restaurant in the Franconia on West Seventy-Second Street where he lived.

Wassel grew up in East Harlem with several guys who later became top members of the Genovese family. When we met, he was an entrepreneur in such diverse businesses as merchandise liquidation, music, and bookmaking.

In an interview with *Vanity Fair* in December 2000 titled "Hipsters and Hoodlums" by Nick Tosches, Wassel recounts an incident involving a disc jockey who accepted payola but never put the record on the air: "So there's this disc jockey and I'm looking at him, and he's, like, this little midget. I throw open the window, pick him up, flip him, shake him out by the ankles. Ninth floor."

Wassel was also known to have hit Van Morrison over the head with his guitar because of the performer's bad behavior.

CHAPTER 20

SOME MORE FRIENDS

In my mind, two men qualified as true friends (in the more traditional, personal way that we think of friends) to my dad.

Alan Sherman from Oceanside, Long Island, was perhaps my father's closest friend. I met him and his wife, Liz, in the late 1970s while on a junket to the Dunes Hotel in Vegas. Alan would spend endless time with my dad and was frequently subjected to my dad's nonstop kvetching or complaining about us, business, the state of the union, and so on. My father loved Alan and counted on him.

James "Jimmy" Cataldo appeared on my father's friendship scene later than all the others. He was probably in his late forties when I first met him and his twin brother, Sal, in the early 2000s. Both men were very overweight but packed solidly from a lifetime of heavy manual labor. Their fleshy faces had warm smiles, and they were both friendly, respectful, and anxious to please. They were in the preowned restaurant-supply-equipment business, and despite their hard work ethic, stamina, and physical strength, they lacked business sense. Always on the lookout for an opportunity, my dad hoped that an infusion of money and brains might make a success of the business, so he accompanied the brothers to equipment auctions, learned what to buy, how to price it, and whom best to sell it to.

More than once, I saw my father's eyes bulge out in anger after Jimmy had done something in the business that my father thought was wrong, but it always passed. They were like father and son. You will later learn more about their business ventures and how each proved his devotion in very difficult circumstances.

CHAPTER 21

WHAT WAS IT ABOUT JOHNNY?

Prior to my getting the subpoena and appearing before the grand jury—that is, before I was forced to look at and acknowledge my father's role in organized crime—I tried to analyze why my father was so well liked by so many influential people. It had been very easy for me in the past to note my father's flaws, but after spending time with him, I started to acknowledge and admire his strengths. What was it about this man that enabled him to befriend movers and shakers in such a variety of industries?

I had been told that it was a big mistake to judge John Novick by either his appearance or his speech. On the outside my father was a schlub, overweight and sloppily dressed. I would tease him that he dressed like a homeless person. He had big, strong, hairy arms and a massive, solid stomach. He wore short-sleeved, XXXL, collared shirts with logos (mostly freebies) regardless of the weather. Unless a shirt was making its debut, it was most often spotted with an assortment of food stains that no amount of washing could remove. His pants, threadbare and shiny from constant wear, hung limply around his legs and pooled at the tops of his shoes. A belt, buckled underneath his enormous gut, would pull his pants so tightly that the material would usually be embedded in the crack of his behind.

My mother would say, "John, for Christ's sake, pull the pants out of your ass!"

He had a few favorite pairs of shoes that he wore until they practically disintegrated: a black pair of sneakers (often paired with white sports socks) and a reddish-brown pair of pleather slip-ons, which my mother named "his Aladdin shoes" because the toe area had curled upward over the years.

Though my dad used lots of slang and mispronounced many words, his malapropisms were humorously endearing.

On a 1970s family vacation at the Doral Hotel on Miami Beach, I listened as he chatted by the pool with the woman in the chair next to him about the thousands of man-of-war fish bobbing on top of the ocean. To my horror, my father explained to her, "Those creatures can do a lot of damage. They wrap their testicles around ya, and it can be very painful."

The woman politely excused herself from the conversation, took her towel, and found another chair.

During the same vacation, the smaller hotels on the beach all began to post signs welcoming their French Canadian guests that read Welcome Bienvenue. While driving around one evening after dinner, my father asked my mother and me, "Who is this Bienvenue person that everyone is welcoming?"

***

In Peter Luger Steak House on Long Island one evening, my parents ran into an old acquaintance, a jeweler and his wife, whom they hadn't seen in decades. My father, with all his tact, said, "Son of a gun [a favorite saying of his], it's good to see you, Joey. It's been a long time. I never knew that your wife is Chinese."

Joey and his wife were dumbstruck. My mother was in disbelief as she swiftly ushered my father away from their table with quick goodbyes.

"Johnny, I don't know what I am going to do with you. You're certifiable, do you know that? The woman had a bad face-lift! She is not Chinese!"

* * *

While on a taxi ride in Curaçao in the early 1970s, my father used his diplomatic skills to get to know about the island and the driver's life by asking him a series of personal questions. Dad used his version of universal language to carry on a conversation: "You build house? You have family live in house? How much money you make?"

My mother, never able to miss an opportunity to zing my father, responded, "Oh my God, Johnny! What's with that way of talking? Who do you think you are, Tarzan? All these questions! What's your business? Why don't you ask him his blood type?"

The driver was clearly bewildered, though not from a lack of understanding. He spoke English beautifully, and we all had a good laugh.

* * *

Despite all initial outward indications of him being a large moron, John Novick was disarmingly smart. To presume otherwise could put you at a disadvantage. Lawyers, doctors, and business executives were amazed that this guy in the Members Only jacket who often mispronounced words knew so much about so much! He read several morning newspapers religiously and was on top of both national and international politics. He followed the stock market daily and drove his brokers crazy with incessant calls to monitor his investments. He was brilliant with numbers, which was why he was such a good card player. You could feed him statistics about a business, and he was able to calculate in his head whether it would be viable in a year's time. If you owed him money, you could count on him to remember the exact amount until you paid, even many years later.

Dad was a product of the streets, which often gave him a unique advantage over those formally educated. He could read people's character fast and furiously and then sentenced them to either the discard or keep pile depending on their usefulness to him. I didn't like many of his choices for friends and business associates, but it was apparent that each one of them served a purpose. It wasn't a matter of "using" people; it was more like a banking system: you kept depositing people into the account knowing that someday they would be needed and drawn upon—a lesson from the streets.

This quality was particularly difficult for me to handle because he sized up my friends, my boyfriends, and even my life situations quickly and without mercy. He rarely kept his thoughts to himself, which stifled my ability to make judgments of my own. I tended to accept what my father thought without giving myself the time to make my own determinations; it was often just easier to let him decide things for me. It also gave me a scapegoat; if someone or something didn't work out as I had hoped, I was able to exonerate myself of any blame.

John Novick was also a loyal friend. He gave advice, whether solicited or not, and had a strong opinion on just about everything. When he was done sharing his views, no matter how contrary they were to yours, you gave them consideration. I heard him mediate disputes between wiseguys and people who got mixed up with the wiseguys, as well as friends who were in disputes with either the law or their business partners, or friends who had problems with their wives and girlfriends (sometimes both). In 2009, months before he died, I saw him resolve a disagreement between two of his friends who were threatening to go to court. From his hospital bed in rehab, he met with each man individually and then together to give his decision on how the situation would be handled.

The older I got and the more time I spent in the company of my father, his friends, and his business associates, the more I understood the real root of his power: his connection to those in organized crime gave him access to opportunities, while his smarts and his big balls gave him the ability to make the most of those opportunities.

My dad was everyone's go-to man, from the smallest of favors asked to the largest of introductions required. Need a good criminal lawyer who was seemingly inaccessible? Not to worry, he'd make the arrangements. Tickets and backstage passes to a Rolling Stones concert at the Garden? If you were willing to pay, he could make the arrangements. Want to get your new store a lease in the mall? He had the guys who could take you to the head of the waiting list. Reservations for the hot downtown restaurant that no one could get into? What time do you want to go, and for how many people? Need money? There were several ways that he could arrange for you to get some. Union problems? He'd see what he could do.

His confidence and fearlessness were a magnet for the weak, the unsure, or the desperate. He offered a solution to everything. To those more cautious, steadfast, or conventional, his behavior could be considered frighteningly reckless and impulsive. I spent a good part of my life vacillating between his versions of reality, leaning on whichever of his shoulders I found most expedient.

Though so much of my anxiety was the result of my father's behavior, I found him remarkably helpful at comforting me with my problems that didn't involve him.

Whenever I expressed to him that I was scared that I would never meet someone, he would say, "Don't worry, there's a cover for every pot."

Angry over the way some boyfriend broke up with me? "He's half a wheel, Lisa. He's crazy. You don't need him. Mommy and I never liked him."

Nervous over a pending medical test result? "A coward dies a thousand deaths." Or "The day you are born it is written the day that you'll die. It is what it is, Lisa."

Feel like playing the "woe is me" game? My father might help put life in perspective by explaining, "If everyone put all of their troubles in an envelope and hung them from a tree for the taking, I guarantee it, Lisa, you would still pick your own."

Deciding whether to get back with a boyfriend in a dead-end relationship? My dad quashed all my doubt with his own version of finality: "You gotta pretend that he died, Lisa. He went off to war and he got killed. There is nothing to go back and forth about in your mind because he's dead! Now stop being so sad. Let's grab a slice of pizza."

Didn't like how someone treated you? "Water off a duck's back, Lisa. What do you care? Forget it, they don't mean a thing to you. Put it out of your mind. Ya feel better now?"

There was a simplicity, almost a childishness, about his life philosophy, but it was very effective.

CHAPTER 22

THE GARMENT
CENTER

I graduated from Columbia in May 1982 with as little direction as when I had entered two years earlier. From the terrace of my apartment in Fort Lee, New Jersey, I often watched container ships traveling on the Hudson River and got it into my head that shipping would be a good industry for me to work in. I applied to US Lines, a container shipping company, and was accepted into its training program. I was told that I had done a stellar job in both the operations and sales parts of the program, and by all accounts, I was primed for a career in the industry. But then something happened—I panicked and left.

With no prospects for a job, I decided to accept my dad's offer to work for him at the ladies' suit company that he had opened in the Garment Center. You might be thinking, *The garment center? How did your father wind up there from the pretzel business?* Good question. But this was the 1980s, and my dad was all over the place putting together all types of business deals, searching for the one that would make him and his backers rich. The deals were all similar: find people who are already established in the industry but who needed money to start or continue a business. Dad arranged to give the money, and then Dad got control of the business. A setup rife with problems!

The idea for the ladies' suit company, Chevaux (French for "horses"), was brought to my father's attention by Jerry and Leo, middle-aged garmentos whom my father had known for years from the sports gambling world. Both men had long, up-and-down sales careers in the garment center and, like other old schoolers, were desperately trying to maintain their place in an industry that was being drastically transformed. They were schmoozers personified, talking to everyone, flirting with the women buyers aged eighteen to eighty, and making deals in the coffee shop with a handshake and the understanding that "you wash my hands, I'll wash yours." They dressed like they were broke, and according to the conversations that I used to over-hear between them and my father, they usually were.

Leo and Jerry had a foolproof, get-rich-quick scheme to copy women's designer suits (which were all the rage in the early 1980s) and produce them inexpensively. They kept over-head at a minimum by renting space in an old building on Seventh Avenue that served as their showroom and warehouse. They would be the salesmen, and another friend (another gam-bler named Bernie) would do the production work for a low price. Bernie was a sweet but nervous guy, and his condition was invariably made worse when in the company of my father. They hired an Indian guy named David (with a suspect long pinky nail) to handle the shipping. Eventually I came onboard and joined the motley crew, because I didn't know what else to do. Leo and Jerry were not happy with me, their new col-league. They knew that I was a set of eyes and ears for my father to keep track of the shenanigans that the desperate pair were known for, like selling clothes out of the showroom for cash and then pocketing the money.

The team did make nice suits, knockoffs of their more expensive Fifth Avenue relatives. By all accounts, my father should have made money, but for some elusive reason, he didn't. We were all out of work.

***

The next attempt at garment greatness was another brain-child of Leo and Jerry's. They introduced my father to Bernie's friend Rita, who had been a designer in the industry for many years. Their proposal was to produce large-size "designer" dresses, a concept that was just beginning in the early 1980s. Manufacturers were realizing the huge, untapped market of women who were larger than a size 12 who wanted or needed to dress as smartly as their smaller-sized sisters. Boutique stores solely for large sizes were springing up around the country, and department stores were starting to dedicate prime space to the larger-sized woman and her dollars. We were at the forefront of a boom. It was ours for the taking, and yet we found a way to fuck it up.

Rita was a gently elegant middle-aged woman whose persona was upper-class continental by way of Brooklyn. She dressed beautifully; had a lovely, soft demeanor; and liked the finer things in life. She had come upon hard times by the time she was introduced to my father, and it was apparent that being in the company of a man like him, let alone being his business partner, was the bottom of the barrel for her. She attempted to use a soft-spoken, rational approach (with a smidgen of flirtation) in her dealings with my dad, but it was wasted. She would sit opposite him, her reading glasses in hand, madly waving about to punctuate her important points.

"John, you have to understand that I will need a nice showroom to welcome the buyers and show the clothes. I will need nice fabrics, as I have a vision of the types of dress lines that

I would like to create. I will need an experienced seamstress to make my patterns, and I need Bernie to make the finished product. I will need a well-established salesperson to get my creations into the stores."

I was in on one of the early group meetings, and I remember the strange dynamics of the partnership. My father was surprised that neither Rita nor Bernie had any money to contribute; they were offering only their expertise to get the business off the ground. On top of that, Rita needed a salary, since that would be her only income. You didn't have to have a Harvard MBA to realize the danger in this kind of setup. My father had to bankroll the whole operation. If it failed, Bernie and Rita walked away clean and John Novick was left with the cleanup. But Rita did have talent, Bernie did have an existing production company, and my father did have money (someone else's?) to invest. I remember Dad saying that they should be a success if everyone did their part. He told everyone that he "had the garment truckers," whose reduced rates would play a significant role in their bottom line.

So, they rented space in 498 Seventh Avenue, which consisted of a small showroom and a tiny production room, with plum-colored carpeting throughout. Rita made herself a private office by closing off an alcove with some leftover silky fabric. My father brought in (from God knows where) mismatched old furniture. There were two desks, one for me and another for a salesperson. For the buyers to view the line and write orders, there was a couch with two glass-and-chrome tables complemented by the ever-popular Breuer chairs. Rita looked like she was going to have a stroke when she saw the decor, but she quickly realized that not having a monetary interest in the business left her at a severe decision-making disadvantage.

The first six months proved encouraging. The initial capital outlay paid for salaries and the fabric needed to make Rita's impressive sample line. Leo and Jerry came through on their promise to provide the buyers, and the giants such as Bloomingdale's, Saks Fifth Avenue, Lord & Taylor, Belk, and Macy's all left orders. The problems began shortly afterward, when the orders had to be filled. My father, not knowing anything about how the Garment Center worked, didn't anticipate how far his money would go. Start-up costs were of course anticipated, but it seemed to be a very long time before any money was coming into the business other than by way of my father.

Bernie's production also proved to be problematic. It was not uncommon for us to receive an entire batch of dresses with uneven hems, seams that did not match up, necklines that didn't lie flat, and zippers that refused to do their job. Perhaps the worst (and the funniest) screwup involved the sleeves of a long-sleeved evening dress. What should have stopped at the wrist extended to the end of the fingertips. The dresses looked like they had been designed for Morticia Addams! We all knew that heads would roll because of the costly screwup, but the sight of the fitting model in the dress was just too ridiculous for us to believe. Even I joined in to brainstorm how to correct the mistake without my father finding out.

As money got tight, our weekly meetings became heated. Rita tried to placate my father with explanations, my father screamed, Bernie shook, and I sat there bewildered. My father made the decision to relieve Bernie of his production duties, to limit Rita's dress line to a few pieces, and to boost sales by hiring someone who was experienced and could work with me so that I could be an asset . . . I had not been an asset.

***

Friends in the industry had learned that Nobert, a six-foot-five, eighty-year-old, suit-and-tie-wearing, stereotypical WASP was looking to make a few bucks by coming out of retirement and

working part-time. He told my father that he had a solid reputation in the dress market and had maintained his relationships with all the prominent buyers in the majors. My father
let Norbert know what was expected of him, and then Norbert
let my father know what he expected of all of us. He had no
reservations about telling us that nothing was to prevent him
from going out for lunch every day and that he had a cocktail
every afternoon at four o'clock. We later learned that he ren-
dezvoused with his girlfriend, who was in her late eighties and
was a dead ringer for Miss Havisham from *Great Expectations!*
My father asked Norbert if he planned to leave the office for his
drink, to which he replied, "Of course not, I will keep a bottle
of vodka and vermouth by my desk. I assume you have a refrigerator here for olives?" *Pinch me,* I thought.

I couldn't believe my dad's reaction. I would have bet that
he'd have thrown Norbert's saggy old ass straight out of the
office, but he didn't! He hired him! *Are we all going insane?* I
wondered. *Is this the person who is going to teach me the business?* The guy looked like he was embalmed, and besides, he was
clearly an experienced bullshitter and had an alcohol problem.
Was my father not seeing the obvious, or was Norbert a last-
ditch effort to save a sinking ship?

Norbert and I did not get along at all. He hated me, and I
hated how he used his tongue to push his dentures in and out
while he was sitting at his desk. I also resented how he was
always trying to get information out of me about my father.
One afternoon when it was just him and me in the office, he
asked, "I hear that your father is very good friends with Benny
Eggs. Is he? I heard that they are big gamblers together in
Atlantic City."

I shot back, "Norbert, my father will be here soon. Why don't
you ask him yourself?" That was the end of that conversation.

Norbert's career with us ended abruptly one afternoon
when UPS delivered a stack of boxes from Saks Fifth Avenue.

As I began to open the boxes, I saw that he was getting very perturbed, and it appeared that he might need his cocktail a few hours earlier than usual. It seemed that sly Norbert had been selling all the dresses on consignment! The dresses were not returned because they were damaged; they were returned because they didn't sell in the stores! Norbert got the buyers to commit to large orders with the understanding that they could be returned if they didn't sell—a disaster for us! After my father tied Norbert onto the torture rack to get him to tell the truth, he admitted that all his sales to the department stores were based on consignment. So, Norbert packed up his pens, pads, and vodka bottle and left our office. The only thing that could be done with the dresses was to sell them to jobbers or discount stores who bought them at pennies on the dollar. Though my father was furious, I wasted no tears on Norbert. I said arrivederci to Norbert and tossed his olive jar into the wastebasket.

My father had reached his limit with money and patience. He had run the gamut of ideas to make the business successful, but nothing took. It was time to close up. One morning, weeks after we no longer went to the office, I arranged to meet my father there to clean out whatever we needed to take before an official closing. When I arrived, there was a Marshal's Notice of Eviction sign posted to the glass door of the showroom. I was still able to get into the office and phoned my father in a panic asking him how far away he was from the office. He was very far; in fact, he had not left the house. He wasn't coming to meet me. He had decided not to come into the city. His last words to me on the phone were, "Take whatever you think we might need and get out of there!"

What! Not understanding how an eviction worked, I was terrified that I would be arrested as I grabbed up the checkbooks, the correspondence, and whatever documents I could find. My father couldn't understand why I was so nervous. As usual, I was told to stop being ridiculous and to do what I had to do. Thinking back, he must have known that we were about to be evicted; he just didn't want to deal with it. He left me alone to clean up the mess.

***

I worried about my next move. I had learned very little in my two-year stint as a "garmenta." There was no way that anyone else would have hired me; I had given minimal effort to learning the business. As with many of my endeavors, I started out with vim and vigor and then gradually lost interest. In my defense, it was a very difficult environment in which to learn. The office was very tense as a result of my father's rants, no matter how justified. I already suffered from rather severe anxiety, and the business only made things worse. I knew that I had to get a job with no connection to my father, but my self-esteem was at a low, and I was once again without direction. Additionally, in my midtwenties I was preoccupied with my social life, which unfortunately distracted me from getting myself established. My difficult relationship with my parents made me desperate to find someone to marry in the hopes of freeing myself from our codependence.

CHAPTER 23

ATLANTIC CITY

In 1976 gambling became legalized in New Jersey. Atlantic City was a natural draw for my dad and Benny because they could have the gambling thrills and luxuries of a junket to Vegas without having to travel across the country. On a good day, Atlantic City was a two-hour limo ride from the city and a forty-minute helicopter ride from Midtown Manhattan, both provided by the casinos to its high rollers. My father would call it a "hee-li-o-copter" despite my mother's efforts to educate him.

"Look, John, you sound like a halfwit," she would say. "Just say that you're going on a chopper! Okay?"

The proximity to home enabled them to take numerous weekend trips to Atlantic City, where they were VIPs at either the Golden Nugget, Trump's Castle, or the Tropicana.

The most time that I ever spent with Benny Eggs and Little Johnny was when I joined my parents for trips to Atlantic City. A private limo would pick me up at my apartment in either Fort Lee, New Jersey, or Manhattan to drive me to Atlantic City, or I would meet my folks at the heliport on East Thirty-Fourth Street. I never took to gambling even though my dad tried to teach me about the games and would give me money to "have fun." For me, fun was traveling or shopping, so I pocketed whatever I was given. I spent my days taking walks on the seedy boardwalk, reading, going to the pool, or watching TV in my room. At night I would meet my folks along with the Manganos and Barbatos for delicious dinners in the gourmet restaurants.

In Atlantic City, as in Vegas, Dad was never in a rush to leave the dining table for the gambling table. He knew that there would be plenty enough time to lose his money. At Lily Langtry's Chinese restaurant in the Golden Nugget, Dad held court as we ate double orders of shrimp and lobster Cantonese, special wonton soup, ginger sea bass, and steak kew with fresh vegetables. Meals were paired with bottles of champagne, expensive wines, and endless pots of fragrant jasmine tea. Desserts were elaborate ice cream concoctions or cakes and pastries brought in from the continental-food dining room. The maître d' fawned over my father, anxious to satisfy his every gastronomical whim.

People would often come over to our table to say hello; some I knew, and others to whom I was introduced. Many would ask my father for favors like getting them a room at the hotel, a line of credit, or show tickets. He never minded; he truly liked to help people, and his ability to procure their requests was a big ego booster. Besides, Dad had no problem asking for a favor in return when he needed it.

Benny had a very different approach toward our dinners; he and his family were there for the gambling, not the food. He hated the long, drawn-out meals my father orchestrated and would often leave for the casino before dessert was served with a parting line such as, "Hey, Novick, when are ya gonna get up from the table? You gonna bust all over us if ya eat another thing! Get your fat ass up from the table already!"

Benny had a great sense of humor, and he was one of the few people other than my mom and me who did not hold back when it came to making fun of my dad's eccentricities.

The VIP treatment at the Golden Nugget was arranged courtesy of casino host Charlie Meyerson. In 1980 Charlie was sixty-four-years old, tall, handsome, and perennially dark-tanned when Steve Wynn approached him to fill the slot as casino host for the newly opened Golden Nugget Hotel in Atlantic City. Steve Wynn knew Meyerson through his father, Michael Wynn, who was a compulsive gambler. Charlie had been his bookie.[35]

Charlie was known to have connections to the Genovese family. As described in John L. Smith's book *Running Scared*, many of Charlie's VIP customers at the Golden Nugget were mob guys to whom he personally granted gambling credit, a violation of New Jersey's Division of Gaming Enforcement regulations. One of these preferred guests was my father, "John Novick, a New York pretzel manufacturer described by gaming investigators as an associate of organized crime, who gambled up to $50,000 each time he visited the Golden Nugget as Meyerson's guest."[36]

In 1986, when Charlie testified before the Casino Control Commission, he was asked how he knew so many mobsters, such as Benny Eggs and Johnny Barbato. Charlie answered that John Novick had provided the introductions.[37]

I found Smith's book on my parents' bookshelf in the early 2000s and was horrified, having never before seen anything about my father in writing. Whatever I suspected or knew was in print for everyone to see. My father had nothing to say when I approached him about the book other than he had no control

---

35. Christopher Smith, "Clash of the Titans," *New York Magazine*, February 16, 1998.
36. John L. Smith, *Running Scared: The Life and Treacherous Times of Las Vegas Casino King Steve Wynn* (New York: Barricade Books), 130.
37. Smith, *Running Scared*, 131.

over what somebody had written. By my next visit to their home, the book had vanished from the shelves.

My mother passed her time in the afternoons feeding dollar coins to the slot machine. At night she would join my dad at the blackjack table, but mostly she loved the one-armed bandits. And bandits they were! She was upset when the new, faster digital machines replaced the older ones that required you to deposit each coin individually into the slot. The old method was slower, so your money lasted longer.

One afternoon I was with my mother at a slot machine as it lit up and the bells starting ringing to signal a big win. As the half-dollars came whooshing out, I reached in and began funneling some of the winnings into my own bucket. We were both laughing as she tried to stop me from taking her loot by hitting me with her cane. When that didn't work, she stood up, threw her body over the machine to protect the spoils of her hard work, and screamed, "Security! Someone get security!" We were never a shy family.

The slots were my mom's one indulgence; she had always been frugal with money. Unlike many of the women in our neighborhood, she was not a big clothes shopper, had no interest in how our house looked, shunned fancy restaurants, and hated traveling. My parents were perfectly content in their lifetimes to have visited only Vegas, Atlantic City, and several of the islands in the Caribbean that offered gambling. My father's travel also extended to the states where he visited Benny in federal prisons.

My mother did have a rather flashy collection of jewelry. My father would find her pieces from either Big Julie or, often while in Vegas, from guys he knew who carried an assortment of pieces in specially made jacket pockets. Quality was not one of my father's discernments; he and my mother opted for the "wow" factor. My mother's sole weakness was cars; she loved a new Caddy, and she always had one with her initials painted on the driver's side door.

I learned in later years that because of my father's gambling, my mother lived with a constant fear of not having money. Her fears were not unjustified. My father's lifestyle did not include conservative investments or insurance policies. She considered her jewelry gifts to be her security and chose to keep them in the vault rather than wear them. She used only part of the money that my father gave her to gamble while in Vegas or Atlantic City; the rest she held aside so that she would have something to take home. Her winnings, if any, were promptly deposited into her savings account. She told me a story of once having hidden money in her shoe on the plane home from Vegas so that my father couldn't get to it. I laughed at the silly sadness of it, her desperation, which I never understood or appreciated until my father's illness and death, when I was left to sort out our financial situation. My mother understood early on that being married to a compulsive gambler left her constantly vulnerable, and she wisely prepared.

My father frequently asked her for a loan to fund a stock tip or his latest business venture. She would refuse, and there would be a battle. I recently watched the incredibly realistic series *The Sopranos* and was struck by the similarity of circumstances between Carmela Soprano and Janet Novick. Carmela lived in fear of how she and the children would survive if something would happen to Tony. That was a running theme in our house as well.

Win or lose, my father always got as much as possible for his casino gambling money. Before leaving the hotel to go home, he took almost everything in the room that wasn't nailed down. Over the years, he had amassed a trove of kitchen items, courtesy of his numerous room service deliveries, including a full set of mismatched dishes and cutlery, creamers, juice glasses, sugar bowls, toast holders, salt and pepper shakers, and egg cups. He filled suitcases with cloth napkins and tablecloths in pink, beige, and white; hundreds of packets of Sweet'N Low (which he later replaced with Splenda); enough small jars of jam to spread on my mother's toast for a lifetime; towels in every size; makeup mirrors; shoehorns; alarm clocks; and shampoo, conditioner, body lotion, and bath gel to keep us all clean and soft well into old age. The heavy, yellowish Golden Nugget embossed bathrobes were my mother's personal favorite. When I moved her from New York to Florida in 2014, she had thirty-four of them in the guest room closet. For some inexplicable reason, she was very resistant to throwing them out, but I placated her by sending five of them to her new home in Miami.

In addition to these freebies, VIP guests like my parents were always given parting gifts at the end of their Vegas or Atlantic City visits. Over the years, my folks had taken home closet loads of stuff, usually in duplicate, but sometimes in triplicate, including Lalique perfume bottles and candy dishes, Wedgwood porcelain salad bowls with matching salt and pepper shakers, crystal candlesticks, ice buckets and decanters, women's leather and mink gloves, men's wooden valets, and sets of luggage. To those whom the junket had put in the hole for tens or hundreds of thousands of dollars, these tokens of the casino's appreciation were like a giant slap in the face!

There must be some psychological study out there on wealthy people who derive pleasure from acquiring freebies, things that they neither need nor want and could easily buy themselves.

In 1987 both Benny and Little Johnny were placed on the New Jersey Casino Control Commission's exclusion list. My father lost his gambling partners, and from then on, they rarely went to Atlantic City.

CHAPTER 24

THE ETERNAL SEARCH FOR A BARGAIN

Despite the enormous amounts my father spent on gambling, my father's thriftiness had not changed as he got older and more successful. Since his circle of friends in every business got wider, most of our major acquisitions, from furnishings to cars, repairs, and jewelry, were based on his connections rather than our personal choices.

In my midtwenties my father bought me a new car. It is not uncommon for kids and even adults with my background to receive luxury gifts from their parents, who do it for myriad psychological and practical reasons. The foremost reason for such advanced-staged spoiling of one's children is simply because they can. While I certainly understood that my folks were not obligated to buy me anything (let alone an apartment, an education, a fur coat, or a car), I did feel very entitled. Grateful, but entitled. I thought of these gifts as payback, the least that my parents could do for all the misery that they put me through. Right or wrong, that was just the way I felt.

My father had a friend who knew someone at a Chevrolet dealership who offered him a terrific deal on a new car for me. My dad could not pass up the price tag, regardless of whether I might like the car. This type of gift giving happened quite a bit with him; a bargain was a bargain. So, when he proudly brought home for me the boxy, burgundy, bare-bones sedan, I couldn't hide my disappointment.

The car had its maiden voyage that evening. We were going into Manhattan to meet Jackie Leonard, my father's good friend and casino host at the Hilton in Las Vegas, for dinner at McCarthy's Steak House on the east side of Midtown Manhattan. My dad thought it would be a good idea to take the Chevy for a test drive. He hoped that I might feel differently about the car once I sampled it. I drove, and he sat beside me, my mother scrunched into the small back seat.

As I drove onto the Fifty-Ninth Street Queensboro Bridge with its spectacular view of Manhattan's skyline, I smelled smoke.

"Do you smell that?" I asked.

"Smell what?" my father replied.

"Smoke. I smell smoke or exhaust or something. I think it's coming from the car." Just then, smoke started to pour out from under the hood.

"Oh my God!" screamed my mother. "Pull over, Lisa! We gotta get out of the car. It's on fire. It can blow up. Pull over!"

My parents never agreed on anything. If one said it was sunny outside, the other would swear it was raining. But this time they agreed—I needed to pull the car over, and we needed to get out . . . pronto!

I maneuvered the car to the right lane of the traffic-clogged bridge, and the three of us scrambled from the car. There we were, my mother and I, dressed in high heels and our fur coats, standing in the cold on the Queensboro Bridge. A car stopped in front of ours, and a handsome young guy got out to ask us if he could help. I was already thinking that I might be able to make lemonade from this lemon and got into his car with my mom while the men (the poor guy had no clue what his good intentions had gotten him into) decided on how to deal with the stranded car. Since this was before cell phones, we had no idea how long it would take for AAA to save us. Had this Good Samaritan not shown up, we would have had to sit in the freezing cold and wait to be towed while Jackie Leonard would have never known what had happened to us.

Ordinary people, average people, normal people, would have been resigned to their situation, but the Novicks were none of the above. Next thing I knew, we were all in this very nice-looking guy's car headed for the city! My father and I chatted up our driver and learned that he was Jewish, also from Long Island (two gold bars on the slot machine). Then we played Jewish geography and learned that he and I had friends in common (three gold bars! Ding, ding, ding!). He insisted on driving us to the restaurant rather than dropping us off on the other side of the bridge where we could have hailed a cab. We thanked him profusely and pulled up at McCarthy's for dinner only twenty-five minutes later than scheduled.

As for my new car? My father left it on the bridge. He called AAA once we arrived at the restaurant and told them to pick it up and take it somewhere; he didn't care where they took it, just not back to him. The problem belonged to Chevrolet and the guy who had sold him the car.

Days later I was driving a tan Celica hatchback.

***

Our house was furnished by Seymour Weissman Furniture. Seymour was a friend of Dad's from his old Brooklyn days.

We would pick out our furniture from catalogs, and a price was determined. The deals that we received came with concessions, such as a midnight furniture delivery. When my dad complained about a dining room set that arrived in the middle of the night, Seymour replied, "What do you want, John? We had a crazy day. So it's a little late. Look at the price you got!"

Then there was the guy who got us a terrific price on new storm windows for the bedrooms. They looked beautiful, but you just couldn't get them to stay up . . . something about a small, defective mechanism. Then there was the appliance company owned by an acquaintance that sold us the washer and dryer. Laundry time sounded like you were on the launchpad at Cape Canaveral!

* * *

Household repairs were done on a catch-as-catch-can basis. At any given time, at least one of the toilets in my parents' house was broken. Remember Jack, our Israeli neighbor who I am sure at times wished he had never moved into the house next door to the Novick family? Well, Jack was a great handyman, and my father made sure to take advantage of his generous offers to help with any problems. The powder room toilet (a favorite of my father's and therefore a frequent offender) located off the kitchen was always clogged. The conversation between my dad and Jack went something like this during one of the repair visits:

"John, this is the third time that I'm here this month. Are you sure you or Janet aren't throwing anything down here that you shouldn't be? I can't find anything structurally wrong with the toilet!"

My father, pretending to be helpful by hovering over Jack as he peered with a flashlight into the toilet, replied with certainty, "No, we don't put anything down there that we shouldn't, unless Janet is throwing things down there."

A short time later, Jack emerged from the bathroom with two dripping wet pens, "Johnny, are these yours?" My father, not the least bit fazed or apologetic, responded, "Son of a gun! You found my good pens! I was looking for them. Janet, Jack found my pens. They must have fallen out of my shirt pocket when I bent over. Imagine that!"

***

My apartment in Fort Lee, New Jersey, was also decorated by Seymour Weissman Furniture, but the carpet was from another friend, George. George was a very nice man with a lovely wife named Agnes. My father was never able to get her name straight and always called her Angus. She would look at him as if he were deranged.

One afternoon George sent over his guy to install the carpeting in my apartment. During a break, I made him a cup of coffee, and we chatted. As it was the end of the summer, we shared how we had spent the lazy, hazy days. He asked if I'd like to see photos from his vacation with his wife and kids in upstate New York.

"Sure," I said as he handed over a small stack of glossies.

I was not prepared to see quite so much of him and his family. There they all were, at a picnic table, volleyball net visible in the background . . . completely naked! There was my carpet installer in the photo, standing by a picnic table with his long schlong hanging right out there in the neighborhood.

Seeing my surprise or revulsion, he said, "I hope you're not offended? We vacation at a clothing-optional resort. Have you ever been?"

"No, never," I responded. "Would you excuse me for a bit? I'm going to do some work in my room now."

I spent the rest of the afternoon in my bedroom with the door closed. I phoned my mother because the story was just too good to keep to myself. "Ma, I don't believe this!" I said. "Everything, everyone that I get involved with through Daddy is sick! Doesn't that man know anyone normal?"

And yet I never learned my lesson. I continued to involve my father in my purchases right up until he died, knowing perfectly well that no bargain would ever be worth the aggravation!

The biggest disaster came years later when my parents decided to remodel the kitchen and master bathroom in their house. The recommendation for a contractor came from Tony, another friend, who was an insurance adjuster. Tony had survived being shot several times (I believe once in the head) during a robbery attempt at his place of business several years earlier. The contractor just happened to be available to start work immediately! Imagine that!

My parents should have taken equal blame for the fiasco that followed because neither wanted to be bothered to work with the contractor, discuss a detailed plan, pick out fixtures, or supervise the work. Instead, they relied solely on this guy to make all the project's decisions. Behind his back, my mother referred to him as "Dickhead," and what a dickhead he was.

The bathroom remodel should not have come as a shock. The large ceramic floor tiles were glued to the walls and the small wall tiles to the floor, the sink faucets turned on and off backward, the European-style handheld shower apparatus kept sliding down its pole and banging my mother in the head, and the new European toilet was so low to the floor that my elderly parents had to plop themselves down on the seat each time and pray that they would be able to get themselves back up!

The kitchen remodel was also a study in stupidity. One afternoon when I was visiting my parents, I opened the dishwasher to put in a dirty glass. The entire dishwasher unit tipped out of its encasement onto the floor; it hadn't been bolted in!

When my father asked Dickhead why it was left in that danger-ous position, he was calmly informed, "I didn't have the right screws yet."

Weeks later we learned from an article in *Newsday* that Dickhead had been arrested for drug dealing and something to do with prostitution. What a shock! He was not a licensed contractor! You could have blown me away!

***

Dad had a habit of paying bills at the last minute possible or, in many cases, not paying at all. The genteel Italian gardener who came weekly to care for my parents' quarter-acre lawn (the house sat on it) was one of the poor souls who fell into the latter category. Each week Carlo would leave his bill in our mailbox, and each week my father would stick the bill into his bulging unpaid bills folder. Carlo must have heard about Mr. John's background because he was afraid to ask for payment. After many months Carlo would gather up enough courage to phone our house and in very spotty English ask about payment. Imagine how happy, how hopeful Carlo must have been when my father would tell him to stop by the house on a Sunday morning and he would take care of the outstanding bills.

The ring of the doorbell on Sunday morning sent my father flying into the bathroom, leaving my mother to make excuses: "John isn't home now and didn't leave money." Or "Johnny didn't like the way you cut the lawn last time." Or "Johnny has been in the bathroom for the last hour. He has cramps. No telling how long he will be in there. Best if you don't wait." She hated being complicit in this game but had no choice.

I once got so disgusted with my father's treatment of Carlo that I resorted to telling him what the Talmud (the book of Jewish law) says about a Jew being obligated to pay for goods and services that were rendered. You can only imagine how impactful that was!

CHAPTER 25

A HUSBAND FOR ME

I was introduced to my future husband Mark Goldberg in October 1985. After my steady diet of dates who could never have been considered for the role of life partner, Mark arrived in my life like a delicious brownie sundae with many toppings. He was twenty-nine, tall, thin, and unconventionally handsome and had a beautiful smile. In addition, he was Jewish, from Lawrence (one of the Five Towns of Long Island), and was a personal injury attorney with his own up-and-coming practice in Lower Manhattan! *Woo-hoo! A live one!* He was cautious and conservative, the opposite of everything that scared me about my father. His slow-moving gait and rather unenthusiastic personality (his brother, Lionel, later nicknamed him Sparky, a moniker that he surprisingly embraced) belied the fact that he was an accomplished athlete and an award-winning tennis player. Here was a guy who could be considered a mate!

Mark's family was another attraction for me. His mother, Adrienne, was an exotic-looking, vivacious woman who loved spending time with her children and was a dedicated daughter to her parents in Florida. Mark's father had died several years prior, and Adrienne was in the middle of a divorce from her second husband. We instantly liked each other. Mark had a sister, Jane, who was my age, and his brother, Lionel, was five years younger. Mark and his family were the package that I had been waiting for. Photos displayed throughout their house showed a seemingly happy family at the beach, visits with the grandparents, and celebrations to commemorate life's special occasions. I wanted in! I saw Mark and his family as my way out of the chaos of my past and present. Mark told me that the night we met, he said to his mother, "I met the woman that I am going to marry."

For Mark, I, too, was an escape. I was grounded, sensible, and family oriented, even though it became evident early on that my family dynamics were, shall we say, unusual. It was also evident to Mark that my family had money, though the source was suspect. I was living in a lovely apartment on Fifty-Fourth Street and Second Avenue in Manhattan that my parents owned. Mark, who was still living at his mother's home in Lawrence, had to travel on the Long Island Railroad forty-five minutes each day and then take the subway to arrive at his office on lower Broadway. I was well traveled, was devoid of student loans, had coveted connections to get into several of the city's hot-for-the-moment clubs and restaurants, and was generous with the money I had.

Three months after meeting, we were engaged. My parents did not like Mark, and Mark did not like them. A fabulous start! There was little fun in the planning of the wedding and a lot of fighting. My mother was at her worst, right up until the last minute when I asked if I could wear my favorite of her numerous pairs of diamond earrings on my wedding day. I was denied. Her explanation was "You're careless. You'll lose them. No." I wore a pair of costume pearl-and-rhinestone clip-ons.

One of the most entertaining arguments concerned the choice of the invitations. My inner Martha Stewart insisted on a cream-colored linen invitation with engraved printing. Simple and elegant. My father could not understand why I would choose such a boring invitation.

"Lisa, look at this invitation," he said, holding up an oversized lilac-colored invite that was adorned with mirrored discs and tassels. The print was so ornate that it was impossible to read. As they say in Yiddish, it was *ungapatchka*, or very much overdone! "It's for Larry's kid's wedding. Now this is a beautiful invitation! It's got some life, not like the one you picked out. Yours is so . . . so nothing. Why don't you get something like this?"

Another battle involved my father's suggestion that we have entertainment at the wedding. Since those were the days that my father was moving and grooving with the record industry crowd, he thought it would be nice if the Fat Boys (a rotund hip-hop trio) performed for the guests. I thought that Mark would faint at the suggestion, and I was horrified. Dad thought it was a great idea. I threw a tantrum, and no boys, of any size, were mentioned again to perform.

The harsh reality is that we both should have bailed from our union. Our relationship was founded on respect and convenience rather than true love, and we both knew it. We were a spousal mutual aid society, each taking from the other what we needed at that point in our lives. No one was to blame. On December 6, 1986, we got married at the Sephardic Temple in Cedarhurst, New York. Two hundred plus guests dressed in black tie (approximately fifty were from Mark's side) came together to celebrate our nuptials. The gathering looked like the wedding scene in the movie *Goodfellas* when Henry Hill married Karen.

The women arrived in floor-length fur coats that sported big shoulder pads. Their gowns had even bigger shoulder pads and were adorned with every type of glitz imaginable. Hairstyles were consistent with the times, sprayed big and high. The event was an opportunity for the "wearing of the jewels"; the big stuff was taken out of the vault and paraded around for all to ooh and aah over. The men wore black tuxedos, many with their hair also carefully coiffed big and high. I later learned that bodyguards were present throughout the evening, but I never found out if my father had made that arrangement or if they had accompanied a guest.

Mark was good friends with an enormously wealthy couple who lived at one of New York City's most prestigious addresses on Fifth Avenue across from Central Park. Earlier in the year, they had met my parents at the engagement party that they graciously hosted for us at their estate in Bedford, New York. They didn't quite know what to make of my mom and dad, and so they chose to just stay away, as if my parents' gaucheness might be contagious. The video shows the two socialites, in understated formal attire, sitting by themselves at the cocktail party. Their pinched faces had the shared look of "what the fuck are we doing here?"

***

I am convinced that the videographer had a sadistic streak. He managed to capture the wedding's most traditional and touching moments as well as those less so. One clip shows my father talking with a small group of friends during the cocktail hour. When the camera peeks in on their conversation, one of the guys says, "Be careful what you say, this is being recorded."

The video also captures parts of the photo session before the guests arrived. It shows my father in a miserable mood shortly after the telephone conversation he'd had with his mother to determine why she had not yet arrived at the synagogue. I remember doing my best not to cry as I listened to him trying to reason with my grandma Frances, who suffered from dementia.

"Where are you? Why aren't you here?" he screamed into the phone.

"I'm in bed, Hoybit. I took off my girdle and got into bed. The taxi man already came and I told him to go home."

"What? Why did you do that! Get dressed now! Put your girdle back on. The car service will be downstairs in fifteen minutes, and you have to be ready! Lisa is getting married!"

My father was apoplectic, and unfortunately, he felt it necessary to share his feelings with us all. There I was, trying to be calm and give the photographer my best bride smile while having to look at my father's miserable face. Couldn't he have spared me?

The photos show a stressed bride and a terrified and bewildered-looking groom. There are several photos of Mark in which he looks totally out of it. In psychological terms, I believe it is called disassociation. I felt sorry for him. My mother, however, looked calm, happy, and stunning in her white gown and dazzling smile. She had prepared for the festivities—she was on valium.

The rest of the evening went along unremarkably. My parents acted as if they were the hosts of some large party rather than my wedding. They were absorbed with their friends. There was no toast from my parents to Mark and me, and no father-daughter dance. Their behavior was not a surprise, but it still hurt.

***

As was expected, we received lots of envelopes with cash gifts from my parents' friends. The few guests from Mark's side of the family gave us small checks or gifts from the bridal registries of department stores. My father considered these to be cheap and useless, and he made sure that he told me so. He found one gift from a distant aunt of Mark's to be particularly grievous.

"What is this?" he asked while doing an inventory of the nonmonetary gifts.

My mother-in-law, Adrienne, knew immediately that it was a well and tree, a platter used for cutting roasts. The item had carved-out treelike branches and a trunk for collecting the meat's juices.

"A well and tree?" my father said. "What are you going to do with that? You need money, not well and trees! You gotta be kidding! Whoever gave this to you should be ashamed of themselves."

Later, when I tried to return it to B. Altman, they said that it hadn't been sold in the store for at least ten years!

"To be ashamed of oneself" was an often-used saying of my father's and one that I now find myself using. It is, for me, one of the worst things that you can say to someone; it holds you solely responsible for your actions with no room to deny or share. It exposes and humiliates you for behavior that is too awful to even explain. It begs you to look into your heart and soul for atonement. All of this over a fucking brown ceramic well and tree, which I ultimately smashed to bits.

My father used this type of hyperbole as needed to weaken the recipient. It wasn't only me who cringed at comments such as "You should be ashamed of yourself"; I saw grown men take the verbal cut harder than a punch. I knew that my dad was often correct, but to me, his delivery, his timing, always seemed like a deliberate attempt to make me miserable.

I found it very difficult to escape his opinions and constant negativity, which of course affected my relationship with Mark. Becoming Mrs. Goldberg had failed to take me away from Lisa Novick, no matter what was written on my new Social Security card. I couldn't find the safety in Mark that I had hoped would magically occur when we married. My disappointment translated into fear, which made our family's codependence even more destructive.

CHAPTER 26

MAGGIE, MY
DAUGHTER

Margaret "Maggie" Ann Goldberg was born on May 11, 1990, at 12:45 a.m. after I had been in labor for twenty-three hours. My parents, who arrived at the hospital ten hours before the blessed event, were not patient people, and the delay was torture for them. Mark had assured them that everything was fine, but at around nine p.m., my father was certain that something was going wrong, and he took it upon himself to investigate.

He and my mother were not allowed to visit me in the labor room, so he had to sneak upstairs to find out for himself what was happening. In my drug-induced state (none of that natural childbirth stuff for me; earlier I had screamed, "Drugs! Give me drugs! NOW!"), I thought I was hallucinating when I saw a big man who looked like my father standing by the door of my room, mouthing something and waving. Then I saw a nurse at the door, arguing with this man who was refusing to leave. I waved back to the big man, and then he left. I drifted in and out of sleep, dreaming of being ten centimeters dilated.

At around ten thirty p.m., feeling exhausted and even more loopy, I looked up and saw the same large man waving at me and blowing a kiss. Again, I waved back. And then I thought I saw a security guard grabbing the man by the arm and trying to pull him away from my room. Loud voices. An argument?

My father was threatened with eviction from the hospital if he was caught sneaking upstairs again. When I heard the story later, I was very touched.

I had never seen my parents so happy as when they finally saw that I was okay and that their granddaughter was born and was healthy. The next day, to celebrate, my father thought that a pastrami sandwich on rye with mustard and a sour pickle, washed down with a Dr. Brown's cream soda, would be just what I wanted for my first full meal in days. The smell alone was enough to make me sick!

We brought Maggie home from the hospital on a rainy, cold Mother's Day. I knew nothing about taking care of a baby, and I was terrified. Because it is a Jewish superstition not to bring anything baby-related into your home until the baby is born (lest there be a tragedy), I had all of Maggie's furniture and clothes delivered to my mother's house. I asked her to please wash Maggie's coming-home clothes and bring them to the hospital when she visited with my father. To my surprise, she brought the clothes just as they had been delivered to her, in their plastic packing, with all tags intact. I was furious. When I asked her why she didn't wash the clothes, she just looked at me with an expression bordering on satisfaction.

Because Maggie arrived two weeks early, the scheduled baby nurse was unavailable, and I was left to scramble for a last-minute replacement. Her name was Grace, an eighty-two-year-old Jamaican woman who had been a baby nurse her entire adult life. She wore a crisp white uniform and had a rigid job description (no cleaning, no cooking, and no laundry other than the baby's). She was a pro; Maggie and I would be in good hands. I had decided to give nursing a try (to the disgust of my mother), so Grace and I decided that we would both get up for the middle-of-the-night feedings and diaper changes.

With the first crackling sounds on the baby monitor, I jumped out of bed, unbuttoned my nightgown, and dashed into the nursery. Grace, who was asleep in the next room, did not dash anywhere. When I settled into the rocker and Maggie latched on, I quietly called for Grace to come in to help. When that didn't work, I started to tap into the baby monitor, at first gently, then more anxiously. That didn't work either. I finally knocked on her door and peeked in.

"Grace. Grace, wake up. Maggie is up and I need you. GRACE!"

Fearing that this old woman might have expired, I went over to her bed and gave her a poke. When I was finally able to rouse her, she shuffled into the nursery, mumbling something to me about being partially deaf. Did I hear her say "deaf"? We had a deaf baby nurse? She lasted a few days and then out she went. Her replacement was worse. Thanks to the help of my baby-loving mother-in-law and sister-in-law (and a disintegrating copy of Dr. Spock's 1946 classic *Baby and Child Care*), I got a crash course in caring for Maggie.

What I really wanted was my mother. I wanted her to be with me in those early days, even though I knew she was just as clueless as I was when it came to baby care. I wanted my mother to spend time at my house, if only for just a few hours each day, to keep me company, to coo over Maggie, to tell me that my fears, frustration, and loneliness were all normal for a new mother. But she wouldn't. There were no excuses, just a "no" to my requests. When I begged, she told me to get another baby nurse. She knew perfectly well that I wanted and needed *her*. Sadly, this bizarre behavior was another symptom of her illness and a painful reminder that she probably would never be the mother that I hoped for.

My father tried to make amends for his absence in my sister's and my life by being a better grandfather than he was a father. I encouraged his relationship with Maggie any way that I could.

One summer evening when Maggie was three months old and was napping in her stroller at my parents' home, I asked my father to babysit while my mother and I went to the local deli to grab dinner. Maggie was not the easiest baby; she suffered from colic, which later was followed by separation and stranger anxiety. No sooner had I settled into the booth, picked up the menu, and started to engage in deliciously mindless conversation with my mother when Georgie at the deli's desk shouted, "Hey, Lisa, your father is on the phone!"

In a near-panic voice, my father said, "Lisa, you need to come home now. Maggie's up. She's moving. I tried to give her the pacifier, but she won't take it. She's starting to cry now. You and Mommy better come home. Take the food with you."

"Daddy, please. I'm so tired. Just give me forty-five minutes. She is moving because that's what living things do! You can try shaking the carriage or even picking her up and walking with her. You can do it."

We packed up our corned beef sandwiches and went back to the house.

A few months short of Maggie's third birthday, Mark and I split. We had a long, costly divorce that culminated in a two-week trial, largely fueled by my father's anger at Mark. Despite the animosity, at no time did my parents, at least to me and Maggie, ever bad-mouth him. They agreed that no good would come from that tactic. Mark was the father of my child. Since he could not have known this, he lived in fear of a mob-movie-style reprisal against him. For years he "packed" a plastic machine gun with pellets in the trunk of his car. Try to see the humor here!

As a single mom, I spent a lot of time with Maggie at my parents' home on Long Island. When Maggie was old enough to watch programs on TV other than *Clifford* and *Power Rangers*, my father encouraged her to join him in watching football and baseball. Maggie enjoyed both watching and playing sports, and she was delighted when my father took her to games and got her valuable baseball cards for her collection and autographed sports memorabilia.

By the time Maggie turned six, she was ready for the serious stuff. My father taught her how to play gin rummy. They would sit at the kitchen table together, a sports game playing in the background, snacks laid out for nourishment, and stacks of pennies, nickels, and dimes in front of each of them to make the game a bit more interesting. Maggie proved to be very good at gin and gushed from pride.

One day Maggie told me that her father was not happy that she was playing cards for money. "My daddy says that Grandpa is teaching me how to gamble and I shouldn't do it anymore. He said that he is afraid that I will get the gambling sickness like Grandpa has."

I rolled my eyes. M&M's replaced coins.

CHAPTER 27

THE WINDOWS CASE

In May 1990 Benny and fourteen other men from four of the five crime families were indicted in what became known as the Windows Case. Since I had been busy with my pregnancy and then breastfeeding, changing diapers, and learning Raffi songs, I have no recollection of this highly publicized event. The indictment also explains why the Manganos did not go to the races in Saratoga in August with my parents and the Barbatos.

Beginning in the late 1970s, the crime families joined forces to gain control of the New York City Housing Authority's lucrative window-installation business. The mob's influence in the industry was procured courtesy of the Lucchese family, which controlled the Local 580 of the Architectural and Ornamental Ironworkers Union. The mob used bribes and extortion to rig the bids for the contracts, threatening outside contractors with labor problems or property damage if they tried to compete for contracts. The mob placed a "tax" of approximately one or two dollars on every window replaced in New York City's public housing. At the peak, the cartel had in its cookie jar more than $150 million in contracts from the New York City

Housing Authority to install windows in the public housing sector. Benny and Peter Savino, an associate, represented the Genovese family in this moneymaking endeavor.

In 1987 the Feds convinced Savino to become an informant and to wear a wire after he was confronted with evidence implicating him in at least six murders. His information, which ultimately led to several indictments across family lines, led him to spend the rest of his life in the federal witness protection program. He died of cancer in 1997.

The investigation, which had included my appearance in front of the grand jury three years earlier, resulted in the conviction of Benny Eggs; Benedetto Aloi, the consigliere of the Colombo crime family; and Dennis DeLucia, a soldier in the Colombo family.

Of the sixty-eight counts for which Benny was charged in 1991, he was found guilty of only a single charge of labor racketeering.[38]

Federal sentencing guidelines called for three years of prison time, but because of his mob rank and his refusal to cooperate with the government in their investigations, Benny was sentenced to 188 months. His lawyer, Susan Necheles of Hafetz & Necheles LLP, tried for years to get a new hearing, but to no avail. The relationship between Benny and the Feds got even worse when in 1997 he refused to testify against Vincent "the Chin" Gigante. The *Daily News* and the *New York Post* had photos of Benny telling prosecutors, "What do you want to do, shoot me? Shoot me, but I'm not going to answer any questions."

Benny paid the price for refusing to be a state's witness. Despite his failing health, he was bounced around to various federal prisons. My father would fly out to wherever he was placed in order to visit him. Their smiling photos, taken over

---

38. Arnold H. Lubasch, "Window Jury Finds 3 Guilty and Aquits 5," *New York Times*, October 19, 1991.

many years, were always on display on the bookshelves in my parents' den.

CHAPTER 28

LET'S START AGAIN

In the 1990s, with Benny Eggs in prison and the pretzel business sold to the Makkos family, my father, only in his sixties, needed to reinvent himself. This life change meant finding a whole new set of buddies to assist in the transition.

He hooked up with a guy named Jack Pesso, who was involved with the Roosevelt Field shopping mall in Garden City, New York. With Pesso's help, Dad secured three lucrative locations in the food court. The next steps involved finding investors to fund his plans. Since my father either had no money to invest or preferred to use others', he put together an unlikely group of people who had disposable income and who genuinely liked my father and his vision. The group consisted of two doctors (who were good friends of my dad's), the wife of a doctor, and a Long Island builder with dubious credentials. The initial leases in the mall were New York Hot Dog, New York Pretzel, and a grilled chicken spot named Cluckers. My mother and I had a field day with that one!

A guy named Scibelli promised to take my father's companies from the mom-and-pop level to a publicly traded company via franchising, and my dad jumped on board. Scibelli's idea was to "bang open" New York Pretzel and New York Hot Dog stores in mall food courts across the country. My father loved the idea of building the stores cheaply, getting them operational, and then taking the companies public. While admirable in his intentions, my father was often childlike in his lack of consideration of practical concerns and consequences. He was easily enticed by get-rich-quick schemes rather than projects that required the patience and focus necessary for a shot at success.

Our corporate office (and I use the term lightly) was in an office building right outside the Roosevelt Field mall in Garden City. The office was decorated courtesy of my father's friend Jimmy Cataldo. A hodgepodge of desks and chairs were brought in to accommodate the hodgepodge of people who visited the office. A large, damaged fish tank stocked with a variety of fish was the showpiece of the conference room. My father loved those fish! He claimed that watching the underwater scene while he worked was very calming.

***

One of the infrequent and by far the most colorful of visitors to our office in the early 2000s was Anthony Rabito. Anthony was a very large man in his seventies, with a head of thick white hair, a boyish smile, good manners, and a classic Brooklyn accent. I had never heard his name prior to his first visit to the office. As my father was notoriously late for appointments, Anthony and I would chat and get to know each other. Eventually, I asked my mother about Anthony.

"He's a nice guy. He was also a big-time mobster. He might have just gotten out of prison. I'm not sure." *Are you kidding me? Oh my God!* I thought. I put an end to office meetings with Anthony unless my father promised to be on time.

My online research determined that Anthony Rabito was a Bonanno crime family capo and reputed consigliere. In the 1980s he served six and a half years for his role in a prescription drug ring that sold large amounts of Vicodin on the street.[39] The drug charges resulted from the work of FBI agent Joe Pistone's (Donnie Brasco) infiltration of the Bonanno family. In a taped conversation, one of Rabito's underlings was heard saying, "Anthony is as serious as cancer. He's a stickler for fuckin' things. Don't underestimate that fuckin' guy 'cause he's got a cane . . . He's an old, old hoodlum. He really is."[40]

In June 2005 Rabito was one of twelve men indicted for mob-related illegal gambling. Rabito profited from the gambling operation by offering the Bonanno family's protection in exchange for money. In 2006 Rabito was sentenced to two and a half years in jail. He was released in 2009.

When Rabito was released from prison, his probation officers prohibited him from going to the restaurants in the boroughs that were known mob hangouts, including Bamonte's, Don Peppe, Rao's, and the Parkside Restaurant. When reporters asked him for a response, he said, "I ate at them my whole life." But, he added, "It'll save me some money."[41]

Apparently, the funny, charming Anthony Rabito whom I had met had an evil twin! He stopped coming to the office and was never mentioned again by my father.

***

The mall businesses were a mess, plain and simple. Mr. Scibelli's plan to bang open New York Pretzel stores in malls in Louisiana, Connecticut, Ohio, and New York City was costly

---

39. United States v. Ruggiero, 726 F.2d 913 (2nd Cir. 1984).
40. Stefanie Cohen, "Feds Say: Fugedabout-eat," *New York Post*, August 2, 2009.
41. Cohen, "Feds Say: Fugedabout-eat."

and neither well planned nor executed. The most glaring problem involved the lack of management; my father had no one to oversee these stores! He micromanaged them by getting stuck on the insignificant details at the expense of the larger picture. We had no long-term plans; everything was done on an ad hoc basis depending on cash flow.

Our New York Pretzel store in the food court of the Roosevelt Field mall was a big moneymaker but could have been even more successful with the right kind of management. The stores were literally thrown together with the cheapest construction and equipment and thus suffered from numerous repair issues. New York Hot Dog shared the same fate: constant problems. At one point my father tried desperately to revive falling sales by offering any type of food that he could procure, often ignoring the mall's exclusivity rules. New York Hot Dog started to look like the dollar store of the food court, disparate items for sale including hot dogs, churros, sandwiches, breakfast items, frozen drinks, candy apples, and more. We were desperate, and the place looked like it!

My father and I fought constantly in those years that I worked in the office. I found the lack of structure unworkable and lost interest very quickly. My father was not open to suggestions on how to improve things. After a lifetime of fighting with him and trying to make myself relevant, I accepted my limited role and just gave up.

My father was forever pumping fresh money into the businesses to keep us afloat. One afternoon a supplier came into the office to pick up a $15,000 check that he had been promised.

"Lisa," my father shouted to me at my desk in the front office, "write a check to Tony for $15,000."

"No problem, Dad," I shot back. "Which account would you like me to write the check from, the one with negative $115,000 or the one with negative $75,000?" My sarcasm was not appreciated!

In retrospect, I believe that my dad suffered from ADHD his entire life. With all his connections and opportunities, had he been more centered, more patient in his endeavors, he probably would have been a huge success in business, even with his gambling appetite. Benny referred to his comical business schemes as "pie in the sky" and was correct in pointing out that they were frequently a waste of time and money.

In addition to the mall businesses, Dad invested in, or considered investing in, some of the most harebrained schemes imaginable, including a bonsai tree company, buying and selling obsolete hospital beds from the Philippines, searching for a market to sell a recipe for chopped clams (bread crumbs and mozzarella cheese stuffed into a clam half shell), and my personal favorite, the shoebox venture.

We were alone in our office one late afternoon when he told me about an idea that had been brought to him concerning the buying and reselling of shoeboxes from China. He had me use a calculator to collect the numbers that he threw off the top of his head.

"Let me see. We have four million boxes. Multiply that by .02, which is $80,000, our cost to buy them, and I make four cents on each box . . ."

Dad then followed with seemingly endless round permutations based on his vision of the sales. According to the numbers that I punched in, his investment could yield a net profit of roughly $12 million! Clearly his skill at numbers had tarnished with his age; there was an error somewhere in the plans! I just looked up at him and said, "Sounds like a good investment, Dad. You should definitely go for it." Even he had to smirk.

***

Nowhere was Dad's relentless drive better illustrated than in his relationship with the twins Jimmy and Sal Cataldo. My father's involvement in the restaurant supply business didn't prove lucrative, and the benefits were minimal. For my mother and me, the spoils were unmatched dishes, preparatory and serving utensils, and commercial-sized pots and pans. Since neither of us were big cooks and my home entertaining was geared toward intimate dinner parties, we didn't have much use for sixty-inch paella pans or commercial-sized mixers that were available for taking. One morning my mom noticed that a new set of teaspoons had found their way into her home. The spoons, stamped with the words "Property of the State of New Jersey," were surplus prison cutlery. She lost her appetite envisioning whose mouths those spoons might have gone into. From then on, she refused to allow my father to bring home another piece of used anything!

Dad's friends in the restaurant business did benefit (or suffered) from his new venture, depending on perspective. The Woodro, an old-fashioned Jewish-style deli, was a landmark of sorts in Hewlett, New York. The deli was popular with my dad, his cronies, and other Five Towners who craved such old-time favorites as chicken soup with matzoh balls; kreplach, pastrami, corned beef, or beef tongue sandwiches on club bread; coleslaw and pickles (sour and half-sour); cans of Dr. Brown's soda; and kasha varnishkas. The Woodro was sorely in need of a tightly budgeted makeover, and Dad was on the spot to help it.

My father decorated the aged deli with an assemblage of chairs in various stages of pre-use, some with vinyl upholstery, some with square backs, others rounded, and most with uneven bottoms so that the chairs never sat firmly on the tiled floor. My father was very proud of his role in the deli's sprucing up. My mother and I had a hard time controlling ourselves whenever we witnessed many a large-bottomed patron attempting to get comfortable in their rickety chair. With each bite from the customers' oversized brisket sandwich, the tired chairs groaned in protest.

At hole-in-the-wall restaurants throughout the boroughs, interspersed between several courses of food, my father and Jimmy spent hours together discussing ways to make money. Someone introduced my father to top executives at Foxwoods Resort Casino in Connecticut, which is owned and operated by the Mashantucket Pequot Tribal Nation. The tribal nations are excellent at making money with their casino hotels, and my father had dreams of opening one of our New York Pretzel stores in Foxwoods. He also hoped to make a connection for one of his friends to provide all the portable toilets for the outdoor tribal events such as the annual powwow. I once joined my dad and Jimmy for a meeting in Connecticut with the tribal chief's representative and his advisers (who were also his relatives). These men were no-nonsense, highly professional; no amount of my father's you-are-my-best-buddy charm could change that. We left the meeting with their request for us to provide the chief with a formal proposal, as well as an invitation to the next powwow. My father seemed optimistic—one of his best traits in business, but not one of mine. As the eternal realist, I rolled my eyes and mentally put my moccasins back in the closet.

In the summer of 2005, Jimmy and Sal talked my father into opening a pizza kiosk located on the dock of Kismet, a community on Fire Island. The concept sounded terrific: hungry people getting off the ferry from Long Island could stop for a slice or a pie, hero sandwiches, and cannoli for dessert before going to their homes. Without consulting my dad, Sal went ahead and had two hundred T-shirts with their logo printed as advertisement. He also purchased two large tricycles with food storage boxes to make home deliveries on the car-free island. My father wanted to keep costs at rock bottom, but again, when someone is not using his own money, there is a tendency to be less cautious with purchases.

The venture was a bust before it started. First, there was the twins' constant fighting.

On my only visit to see the place, I heard Jimmy scream at Sal, "I'm going to put your head in the pizza oven!" To which Sal replied, "I'd like to see you try!" This delightful banter was of course audible to any patrons whom they were lucky to have. In 2005, Long Island summer fun was curbed by the arrival of the West Nile virus, which was spread to humans by mosquitoes. Even die-hard beachgoers, scared by the media's warnings, opted to stay within their air-conditioned homes rather than risk being bitten. Beach community businesses suffered greatly. My mother and I jokingly nicknamed the pizza joint West Nile by the Bay.

This parade of get-rich-quick schemes intensified as my father's health sharply deteriorated in his late seventies. His weight blew up as his body filled with fluid, and his heart did its best to keep him going. I knew that his gluttonous eating and his out-of-control gambling were how he dealt with his fears. He never looked inward or dealt with his shortcomings; instead, he gobbled them down in a giant bowl of rigatoni all'amatriciana or a huge porterhouse steak broiled in butter. He was also very afraid of dying. He wanted desperately to score one last business hit before it all ended, but he had neither the energy nor the money nor the patience to make it all happen. I would have loved to have seen him living in a condo in Miami, wearing a cabana suit and playing gin rummy by the pool with friends, but that was my dream, not his. He was like a shark who just had to keep swimming.

CHAPTER 29

IT ALL CAME TUMBLING DOWN

In 2006 Benny Eggs was released from prison and placed in a federal government–sponsored halfway house in Bedford-Stuyvesant, Brooklyn. The conditions were not suited for his advanced age and failing health. He should have been granted home confinement, but supposedly he was still being punished for his refusal to cooperate with the government years earlier. His parole officer would call his home at two a.m. to check on his whereabouts. Benny was eighty-five years old, and Louise, his wife, was very sick; they were not out partying.

When Benny was free to return to his apartment in the West Village, my father would visit him frequently. It was alleged that he still ran the Genovese family's business from the confines of his home. The world had changed dramatically during the years that the old friends were separated. For a start, they were both old. My father turned seventy-eight in 2006, and decades of abusing his body had taken a toll on his health, his ability to get around, and I believe, his ability to make sound business decisions. Alan Sherman would often serve as his driver when he needed to go into the city to meet Benny. A shifting of alliances had also taken place over the past sixteen years of Benny's absence; many associates were jailed, murdered, or had died of natural causes. Mayor Rudy Giuliani's 1980s campaign to clean up organized crime in the five boroughs was largely successful at dismantling the lucrative syndicates. Business was not "as usual" following Benny's homecoming.

While in prison, Benny had become very close with Murray Wilson. My father and Murray often went together to visit Benny at whatever prison he was housed in. One night in 2008, my father went to meet Murray and some other guys at his restaurant, Campagnola. Jimmy joined him, having spent the day driving my father around town. Years later, I was told by someone who was at the dinner that what went down that evening changed the course of Benny and my father's long friendship.

Murray, whose behavior always ran hot and cold, from friendly and gracious to obnoxious and mean, said to Jimmy, in front of everyone seated at the table, something to the effect of "Stuffing your face again, you fat pig? You think that you're going to eat at my place for nothing?"

Jimmy, who was obviously embarrassed by the unprovoked attack, responded, "Go fuck yourself, Murray. I don't need your free food. I can pay for myself."

Everyone at the table was shocked by the cruelty of Murray's comment and then by Jimmy's response. But the real problem resulted from what *wasn't* said. According to some unwritten law of mobster protocol, my father should have strongly rebuked Jimmy for talking to Murray that way. But it never happened; my father stood by him. Murray was furious with my father, and the relationship was officially severed.

Shortly after that evening, my father had a usual meeting with Benny in New York City. My dad was always late for appointments, and his excuses wore thin and pissed off many people. That day was no exception. Supposedly, Benny was particularly annoyed that my father was hours late for their meeting and told him so. That was the last time they ever saw each other after having been best friends for more than seventy years.

Anyway, that was the story for street consumption, but to those close to both my father and Benny, it could *never* have been the sole reason for the breakup. Both men were in their eighties and ailing, and both had put up with each other's idiosyncrasies for a long time. More likely, what happened is that Murray told Benny about the scene at the restaurant with Jimmy and how Johnny Novick handled (or rather didn't handle) things. From what I had seen and heard, Murray was an instigator, and his efforts had hit the jackpot.

Murray died of a heart attack on October 13, 2010, at age seventy-two.

Benny died on August 18, 2017.

***

And Little Johnny? In June 2006 John "Johnny Sausage" Barbato pled guilty to racketeering and extortion charges based on many hours of audio and visual tapes from 2002 and 2003 between him and Anthony "Tony Muscles" Guardino, the boss of Local 8 of the United Union of Roofers, Waterproofers, and Allied Workers. During this time period, the mob, with its power behind the union, took an estimated $110,000 per month in payoffs from contractors. In return for the money, the contractors were promised their lives and a pass from labor unrest.[42]

---

42. Jerry Capeci, "A Strong Case against Tony Muscles," *New York Sun*, January 18, 2007.

While Johnny never admitted to being part of the Genovese family, he did confess to the charges and his role in a criminal organization. He told the judge, "This criminal organization was part of a nationwide criminal organization that operated through entities called families. During the relevant period, I was a member and high-ranking official of one such family. I influenced and controlled the Local 8 labor officials, and Local 8, and benefited financially from the criminal activities of the Local 8 group."[43]

In September 2006 Johnny was sentenced to thirty months in federal prison. I am not aware that my father ever saw Johnny again after he was released on July 3, 2008, at age seventy-four. As part of his parole stipulation, he was ordered to stay clear of his mob-related friends, and my father did not want to cause problems by attempting to speak to or see him. I spoke to Johnny on several occasions during 2009 when my father was in the hospital. He always told me to send his love to my dad. My father understood why Little Johnny didn't visit him, but in a rare expression of emotion, my father told me how much he missed his old friend.

***

And Yay? In June 2005 Frank "Yay" Tramontano was one of twelve men (including Anthony Rabito) arrested for running the day-to-day operations of a gambling and loan-sharking ring. The indictment charged that the illegal sports-betting operation took in more than $10.5 million in an eighteen-month period.[44]

Prosecutors said that when they raided Yay's house in Staten Island, they found $160,000 hidden in a wall behind a

---

43. Capeci, "A Strong Case against Tony Muscles."
44. Corey Kilgannon, "12 Are Accused in Mob-Run Betting Scheme," *New York Times*, June 17, 2005.

television set. He then offered to split the money with the cops and to further discuss the matter "over his table at Rao's," the famous East Harlem Italian restaurant.[45]

I knew that Yay had gotten into trouble; I read the newspapers like everyone else. I knew that my father missed him when he went to prison. He was released from jail after my father had already passed away. I called Yay to welcome him home.

My mom said, "Yay was always a really nice guy. Everyone liked him and everyone trusted him."

* * *

And my dad? In 2015, under the Freedom of Information Act (FOIA), I contacted the FBI and requested any records concerning my father. I received a response that said, "The FBI located approximately 29,000 pages potentially related to your subject." To fast-track the production of information, the FBI sent me just 250 pages, which were heavily redacted and useless to me. This probably was a blessing in disguise!

Despite the company my father kept, he was never indicted and never served time in prison. For this, I have always been grateful. I cannot imagine what would have become of our family without my father, no matter how dysfunctional our relationships. My mother recently shared this story with me about a time in his later life when he did go in front of a judge for sports betting.

"The judge told Daddy that he would have to go to Gamblers Anonymous if he wanted to avoid jail time. He was told that he had to go to some church in Flushing [Queens] on certain mornings. Can you imagine Daddy getting out of the house before eleven a.m. for anything? It turned out that it was one of those Korean churches. When your father went

---

45. Alex Ginsberg, "The 'Goodfogeys'—Grandpas Busted in $15M Loan-Shark and Gamble Ring," *New York Post*, June 17, 2005.

into the basement where the meeting was being held, everyone was sitting on chairs and talking about their feelings. Can you just picture him sharing his feelings? It got worse. The leader told everyone to stand up, get into a circle, hold hands, and recite the Serenity Prayer. Oh, to be a fly on the wall, Lisa! That pushed Daddy over the edge, all two-hundred seventy-five pounds of him. He left. When he came home that night, he said that he was never going back, and he never did. I don't know what happened, how he got out of it, but that was the end of his meetings."

＊

And my parents? Their fighting didn't lessen as they got older. I believe they couldn't live without each other and the fire that fueled them. They were two malcontents, unable to live without each other as their whipping boy.

I often took my father's side when they fought, sometimes because I truly believed that he was right in his argument, other times because I suffered less from his delivery than from my mother's. She was always unable to focus her anger and frustration at my father where it belonged; she thought nothing of dragging me right into the middle of the fray. My choice to align with my father released her venom. "Judas. That's who you are, Lisa," she would scream at me. Or "You're too afraid to speak up to your father, Lisa. You're a mouse. Squeak, squeak." Or "You're just like him, Lisa. The apple doesn't fall far from the tree."

CHAPTER 30

CLOSURE

My father entered the hospital in January 2009 for a host of ailments and spent a year, to the day, going back and forth between the ICU and a rehab center. Jimmy rarely missed a day visiting him, often arriving late at night after his workday and sleeping on the chair by his bedside. He would bring my father contraband, such as Chinese food or a corned beef sandwich, but mostly he brought a sense of normalcy, conversation about the world beyond my father's hospital bed. Of all the lessons, both good and bad, that filtered down to me from my dad, the importance of friendship is among the most precious.

Before my father went into heart surgery, we said our goodbyes, just in case. I cried harder than ever before, knowing that the chances for my dad's recovery were not good. He survived the twelve-hour surgery, but in the following months he began dialysis and was put on a respirator. I was beside him almost daily when he was in a coma and when he came out of it.

In the early, snow-covered months of my father's hospitalization, I sat next to his bed, patting his hand and either praying or chattering on incessantly about whatever I could to help deal with my nerves. We had never spent any amount of time together beyond a dinner or a car ride. Now I finally had my father's full attention.

As the months went by, news anchor after news anchor filled our silence as they reported an endless stream of news from a small, perpetually on television that was perched high above my father's bed. I continued my one-sided commentary on the state of world and local affairs, including the arrest of Bernie Madoff, the fluctuations of the stock market, and the status of our businesses.

By the time the trees had begun to turn green and the days grew longer, my father was able to speak. After three months, I heard his voice again. We continued to watch the news, only now we were able to talk about what we saw. We discussed the starting lineups for the Yankees on opening day of the baseball season, and we picked our favorite horses for the Kentucky Derby. We discussed his prognosis with his doctors and by ourselves. I cried when he slept and tried, not always so successfully, to be jolly when he was awake.

When the summer months arrived, my father's health was progressing. He wanted me to stay at the hospital or at the rehab facility with him for as long as I could, whenever I could. He told me that he needed me to be his advocate with the staff at the hospital and that my company made his day pass more quickly. I was very happy to be able to help him. My mother could not handle the pressure, and she went weeks without visiting him.

I reveled in the attention that he gave me, even though it was greatly compromised. I spent part of almost every day with him, driving back and forth to St. Francis Hospital or the Woodmere Rehabilitation and Health Care Center on Long Island from my home in Ardsley, New York. Nothing was more important than our time together, not the business and not my personal life. I was so glad that my daughter, Maggie, was in college at the time and that I didn't have to feel guilty about never being at home. My life belonged to my father.

We talked about his childhood and his relationship with his parents and his brother, Stanley. We talked about how he met Benny and how he got into the pretzel business and what he thought of my mother when they first met. I asked him if he had any regrets and if he thought he had had a good life. I pushed him to talk about his feelings. Was he sad? Scared? The answers were obvious, but I wanted to hear them.

I would lie in bed at night thinking about what I could bring to my dad in the hospital that would encourage memorable conversation. One day we looked through old photo albums and watched my wedding video on my laptop. We talked about how much things had changed since that day in 1986—which guys were in jail, which couples had split, and who had died. We looked at pictures of my gorgeous mother, his gorgeous wife, and commented on how unhappy her life was. We each complained about how difficult she was to get along with and how her refusal to get help for her crippling anxiety and depression had affected us all. We examined pictures of my sister as a baby, as a teenager, and then as a young adult. And then, when there were no more pictures of her in the album because she had ceased to be part of our lives, we put down the albums and sat quietly together, he in his hospital bed and I in my chair.

When the leaves fell off the trees and the days got colder, my father's condition took a downward turn. His forward steps became less and less, and he became disgusted and felt hopeless. We both knew it was the beginning of the end. Our talks were short and mostly about the urgencies of the moment. When Thanksgiving came, he was too depressed to hear anything about the holiday. He didn't smile anymore when I came through the door to visit him and no longer appreciated my cheerleading efforts.

Our joint frustration and resignation bubbled over one late afternoon in early January 2010. My daddy looked nothing like he had one year earlier. He had gone from over 300 pounds to about 150 pounds. With the extreme weight loss, gone was his huge stomach; signature round pumpkin face; strong, hair-covered arms; and sausage-like fingers. He was skeletal, yellow skinned, and dazed. Worst of all, for me, was his fear, so visceral that it occupied its own space in the room. I had spent a couple of particularly stressful hours with him, and I was exhausted and just wanted to run away from the sadness.

"I gotta go now, Daddy," I said, not looking at him directly. "I have to take care of some things at home." I felt angry words welling up inside, and I didn't want to stop them. "I'm tired and I've got hours of work to catch up on. I wanna get on the road before traffic gets unbearable. I'll be back to see you tomorrow afternoon."

"Don't go now, Lisa," he begged. "Please stay longer." He reached out a bony hand, which appeared overly dramatic to me. I was annoyed. "Please, Lisa. Stay. I'm scared. I would do it for you."

I threw my handbag and my car keys down on the floor, and I turned to him and said, "Oh really? You would do it for me? I don't think so. You didn't stay for me when I was a kid and used to beg you to come home for dinner and watch TV with me. You didn't stay when I was afraid and needed you. The nerve to try and guilt me into staying with you! I have been with you almost every day for eleven months. Look at my face! Do you see how exhausted I am? Back and forth every day from Westchester to Long Island to be with you. And then I go home and try to take care of myself and my things. You would have done it for me? I don't think so."

My father was stunned, as if he could not believe what he was hearing. "Why do you think I wouldn't do it for you? That really hurts me."

"Yeah, well, you really hurt me too," I said.

I didn't want to stop my words. I knew how much they were hurting him, how vulnerable he was, but I continued. "You were never around for any of us. You didn't get it, no matter how hard I tried to tell you. And you know why, Daddy? Because you didn't want to get it! You didn't care. When I was a kid, I wanted YOU! I didn't want money and things, I wanted YOU. Money was the easy part."

In his weak, totally beaten voice, he responded, "It wasn't easy at all, Lisa. It was very tough on the streets, tough to make a living. I'm sorry, I really didn't know."

"You knew, Daddy," I said, crumbling. "I made sure you knew. You made a choice, that's all."

I felt ashamed at myself for starting such a painful conversation when he was so sick. I kissed him on the top of his head, scooped up my things, and left.

* * *

My father died on January 28, 2010, exactly one year after he had been admitted to St. Francis Hospital for high-risk heart surgery. When I got the phone call from a doctor that my dad had been taken from the rehab facility back to the hospital for perhaps the twentieth time, I was in Las Vegas tending to our business. The doctor had told me that my father did not want to be treated anymore, and in his medical opinion, it was best to let him go. I was assured that he would be made comfortable with morphine and that he would die peacefully without pain. I cried hysterically by myself in my hotel room, big, fat sobs of sadness and relief. We were both free. It had been a long, painful year.

I was comforted by the knowledge that I had done everything I possibly could to make sure that he got the best care from those who were treating him. Equally as important, I tried through my visits to ease some of his fears about being alone and out of control.

***

I took the red-eye home from Vegas and arrived at my mother's home early Friday morning. It is the Jewish custom for the deceased to be buried as soon as possible, but because my father was superstitious, no preparations had been made in advance for his death. Despite my sadness and exhaustion, I had to get busy right away to make the arrangements for his funeral. First stop was the funeral parlor in my parents' community to purchase a casket and arrange for the funeral. Then I drove to the cemetery in Valhalla, not far from my home, to purchase a burial plot.

I begged my mother to come with me. I needed someone to comfort me. But not surprisingly, she refused. "I can't handle it, Lisa. You do it."

I had heard those words so many times before, no matter how callous or inappropriate.

I wanted my father to have a traditional Jewish burial. Because we had never had a talk about what he wanted upon his death (superstition always trumped practicality), I did what I wanted for him. In keeping with Jewish tradition, I purchased a simple pine casket. The body should go back to God the same way that it entered the world, ashes to ashes, dust to dust. My father's body received a ritual washing in preparation for burial, and I hired a shomer to watch over his body upon arrival at the funeral parlor. This ancient custom is to ensure that the body is respected until the burial, at which time it is believed that the soul leaves the body. In a Jewish funeral, there are no flowers, and no open casket or viewing of the body.

There was a big crowd at the service at the funeral parlor in Hewlett when we said our final goodbyes to John Novick. For the actual burial, just a few of his closest buddies, my mother, my daughter, many of my friends, and I were graveside. Dad was buried on a very cold, sunny Sunday. I had been warned that the ground might be too frozen to prepare the gravesite, but thank goodness this was not the case. The rich dark earth that was piled into a mound next to the hole where my father would be laid to rest was in sharp contrast to the blinding white snow that covered the cemetery.

The rabbi recited the traditional Hebrew condolence: *"Hamakom y'nachem etchem b'toch sh'ar availai tziyon ee yerushalayim."* (May God comfort you among all the mourners of Zion and Jerusalem.)

The speck of Xanax that I had taken earlier that morning had worn off, and I was left raw and sobbing, but very much at peace.

That night, I prayed to God that my father would watch over my mother, my sister, Maggie, and my half brother, Dennis. I prayed for strength to deal with the scattered emotional and business pieces that my father had left behind. As the years have gone by, I often bypass God and speak directly to my father. *Are you proud of me, Daddy? I'm trying to take care of everyone. It isn't easy to do; you know very well how hard it is. But Dad, I'm finally taking care of myself. Are you watching, Daddy? Are you proud of me?*

CHAPTER 31

I MIGHT BE HAVING A NERVOUS BREAKDOWN!

I observed the Jewish custom of shiva, or mourning, without my mother, for two days rather than the customary seven. On Tuesday, following Sunday's funeral, I drove out to Woodmere to see my mother and to take her out for lunch. We went to the Woodro, which had served as my parents' meal provider and social hangout for almost forty years. After our lunch, when we were leaving, two of my father's friends asked if they could speak to me about something important.

"Lisa, we're sorry to have to ask you this, but you know that your father was still betting on the games while he was sick, and well, he bet the last couple of weeks and he lost," said one of the men.

"So?" I responded. "He's dead. What is it that you want?"

"Well, he always told us that when he dies, you would settle up things with us. He told us that you would do the right thing."

"Are you kidding me?" I said. "You mean to tell me that you continued to take bets from him knowing that he was dying? He weighed one hundred fifty pounds! He was high on all kinds of medication, and you took his bets? He was delusional!"

"Lisa," one of his dear friends said in a very solemn voice, "you know how your father was. You know that all he had left to make him happy was gambling. Actually, he had bet on the Super Bowl game, but we're not going to ask you for that money. We hate to ask you now, but he told us that you would do the right thing."

"I don't believe this! My dad isn't even in the ground forty-eight hours and you couldn't even wait to settle this? Where's the respect for me? For him?"

Respect? Talk about fooling myself! I wrote a check for $5,400 and never again saw or heard from either of my father's "good" friends.

The years following my father's death were extremely difficult, and at times I thought that I would surely suffer a nervous breakdown.

The most head-banging and unfulfilling times centered on my relationship with my mother. In the absence of friends, hobbies, or interests of any kind, plus her decreased physical mobility, my mother relied on me to fill the role of daughter, husband, psychiatrist, friend, and caretaker. She was incapable of drawing boundaries in our relationship, another trait of those suffering from her personality disorder. There was nothing off-limits, no request too inappropriate or unreasonable. I could satisfy her momentarily, but not beyond that. The free-for-all that characterized our relationship created a black hole into which I was constantly drawn. My attempts to help her would usually end in such overwhelming frustration that all I could do was scream. And so, I screamed, a lot. I made up for all the times that I couldn't scream when she hurt me. I screamed because I knew that so many of the fears and faults and inabilities that I despised about her were part of me too. I screamed because I loved my mother and was coming to realize that she was never going to change. I would never be able to save her from herself. I would never have the empathetic, strong, warm, and fuzzy mother of my dreams.

When I told my mother that I was writing this book, her reaction was predictable.

"What's with you, Lisa?" she said. "You seem to always revert to the past. Enough already. For Christ's sake. Let it go! You keep playing the same tapes over and over. The past is the past."

She knew the power that these words had over me and used them to mock me. This was not the first time that we had fought over this topic. Perhaps the "past is the past" when photos of family and friends sit in frames atop pianos and shelves as testimony of happy times. The past can never be the past if you wake up every morning and your heart is banging out of your chest for no identifiable reason. Or you dread your daily trips to the mailbox and seeing unknown numbers appear on your cell phone because you wonder what horrible, life-altering news awaits you. Yes, medication does help to lessen the physical symptoms of the anxiety, but these fears have long made their home deep inside, and an exorcism requires far more work than any pill can handle.

Another major challenge facing me after my father's death was deciphering and then untangling the business dealings that he had left. One of my father's lawyers had described his empire as "byzantine" in its setup and operation. I worked hard to try to understand what he had created, and then I had to work even harder to undo and correct what desperately needed to be done in order to keep things afloat. I had my daughter and my mother counting on me to take care of them, as well as my sister, whom I supported financially even though we did not see each other. The responsibility felt overwhelming. For perhaps the first time in my life, I was forced to rely on my own intuition and skills in order to take full responsibility for my future. There was no Daddy to blame. No Daddy to walk away from when the going got tough. Just me.

I found the process trying and challenging but also liberating. The more decisions I made, the more I trusted myself. I embraced advice from those in the know, took some risks, and called on both the positive and negative lessons with which life had schooled me. While I pride myself on being much more mindful and disciplined than my father when it comes to just about everything, I am often struck by how much he lives within me. I can be impatient, judgmental, impetuous, and bitingly sarcastic, but I try to recognize and fix my Johnny Novick qualities that are destructive to my health or relationships. I am also sharp, compassionate, responsible, and brutally honest. I prize honesty above all; it takes the scariness out of my life and lets others know where we stand with one another. I thank my father in my prayers (and, yes, my mother too) for all that they did for me, no matter how tough the life lessons.

In 2014, when I was fifty-six years old and suffering from generalized anxiety disorder and crippling panic attacks and wanting desperately to maintain a healthy relationship with the wonderful man that I had been living with in Miami for the last four years, I entered psychoanalysis. I had enlisted the help of therapists for decades, but mostly on a crisis-management basis. I was finally ready to make the commitment to delve into and confront my issues.

With the help of a wonderful psychoanalyst and continued weekly appointments, I realized that despite all the ugly in my past, I had managed to take the best of what my parents had to offer and make the most of it. Their unorthodox lessons are part of me. I did what those in therapy do: I looked at my past and my present and the good and the bad and I cried and I laughed and I acknowledged that this apple may not have fallen as far from the tree as I might have liked. But it all was, because it all was meant to be. And it's all okay. I'm okay. Maybe even better than that.

By the way, the wonderful man that I married in 2017, Stanford Blake, is a celebrated, retired circuit court judge who served on the bench in Miami for twenty-two years, sixteen of which were spent on the criminal bench. My father would have loved him!

PHOTOS

The Novicks in 1945 at Stanley's bar mitzvah.
Left to right: Stanley, Frances, Irving, and Herbert.

Freedomland in the Bronx, 1963.

My maternal grandparents, Frieda and Morris Matlick.

*March 1966. My father entering the federal grand jury in
Chicago that investigated mob influence in boxing.*

Dunes Hotel, Las Vegas postcard from the late 1960s.

Las Vegas. Bottom left to right (couples): unknown woman with Jerry (he was murdered in front of his home), my mother and father, Judy and Shimmy, Evelyn and "Uncle Mike" Maione (a member of the Genovese family), and Georgia and Leo Genova.

El Morocco Club party in New York City 1984 for VIPs of the Golden Nugget Atlantic City. Beginning third from the left: me, Steve Wynn, Frank Sinatra, and my mother seated in the black-and-white striped top.

December 1986, my wedding to Mark. From left to right: my mother, Benny, "Big Julie" Weintraub, and Seymour Weissman.

My mother and father. December 1986.

Visiting Benny in prison in 2003. Left to right: Johnny Barbato, my father, Benny, and Murray Wilson.

Me, Maggie, and my husband Stanford Blake. April 2019.

ACKNOWLEDGMENTS

At a dinner party in 2014 at Jane and Al Blake's home, I was introduced to Linda Alexander and her husband Gene Gomberg. After hearing stories about my family, they encouraged me to write a screenplay or book about the wacky Novicks. In 2015 when my husband was recovering from cancer of the tonsil and I had lots of time at home, I began to capture in writing the events and feelings that had stayed so close to me since I was a child.

Navigating the waters of publication was extremely challenging as I am new to the literary community. I was introduced to Roy Sekoff, the founding editor of The Huffington Post, who suggested that I self-publish and connected me to Girl Friday Productions. Alexander Rigby, my special projects editor, guided me through the process. I would like to thank my editor, Kelli Martin, for her direction; she took me to another level of thinking.

I am deeply grateful to all my friends and family who encouraged me throughout the development of the manuscript. Their continued praise made it seem possible.

Biggest thank you to my always-supportive husband, Stanford Blake, for his encouragement, faith, and love. He is the wonderful sequel to my journey.

ABOUT THE AUTHOR

Lisa Novick Goldberg was born in Brooklyn and grew up in the Five Towns on Long Island. She raised her daughter, Maggie, in Ardsley, New York. Lisa received her bachelor's degree from Vassar College and her master's degree in international affairs from Columbia School of International and Public Affairs. She now lives in Coconut Grove, Florida with her husband, Stan Blake. *The Apple and the Shady Tree* is her first book.

Made in the USA
Columbia, SC
04 February 2022

55440022R00167